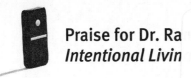

Praise for Dr. Ra
Intentional Livin

D1009504

"The term *intentional living* has made a huge difference in my, the whole mind-set that you start your day with—I'm *intending* to live this way; I'm intending to say the right things, watch the right programs, do the right things—makes a huge difference."

"I have been wanting to live an intentional life, but I didn't know where to start. The Lord helped me start in the area of my finances, which I've been kind of lax at. So I started sitting down and going through each area that I'm paying out every single month (going through my insurance, making changes to my phone, making Internet changes), and so far, I have been able to save $780. I haven't finished yet, but I just wanted to thank you for your help in keeping my focus on being intentional."

"I called quite a few months back and was on the verge of a divorce. You told me to take the higher road and be intentional with my faith and relationship. Then if my husband chose to leave, I would know I did what Christ said. Now our marriage is growing stronger every day. . . . Thanks for your ministry!"

"I tried to quit smoking several times until I realized what I was lacking—it was exactly what I've been hearing on your show, about being intentional. I am three months nonsmoking as of today."

"Since listening to your radio [program], my entire life has changed. I have a different opinion and a different attitude toward how I run and manage my life. I think the intentional living part for me is that I'm finding ways to give back to my community, making that an intentional part of what I do every day."

"I am so thankful for this program. It really helps me stay accountable and live an intentional life. I know that I have my slipups, but I try to do 'one thing' a day and take it from there."

THE POWER
OF ONE THING

THE
POWER
OF
ONE
THING

How to Intentionally Change Your Life

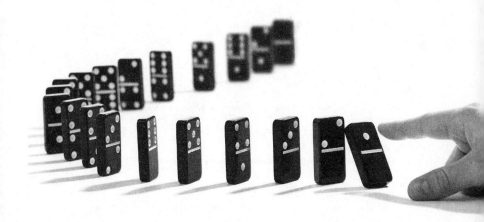

DR. RANDY CARLSON

TYNDALE HOUSE PUBLISHERS, INC., CAROL STREAM, ILLINOIS

Visit Tyndale's exciting Web site at www.tyndale.com.

TYNDALE and Tyndale's quill logo are registered trademarks of Tyndale House Publishers, Inc.

The Power of One Thing: How to Intentionally Change Your Life

Copyright © 2009 by Dr. Randy Carlson. All rights reserved.

Cover photo taken by Stephen Vosloo and Dan Farrell, copyright © by Tyndale House Publishers, Inc. All rights reserved.

Author photo copyright © 2005 by Lance Fairchild Photography. All rights reserved.

Designed by Beth Sparkman

Barbara Kois collaborated in the writing of this book.

All Scripture quotations, unless otherwise indicated, are taken from the HOLY BIBLE, NEW INTERNATIONAL VERSION®. NIV®. Copyright © 1973, 1978, 1984 by International Bible Society. Used by permission of Zondervan. All rights reserved.

Scripture quotations marked NLT are taken from *The Holy Bible,* New Living Translation, copyright © 1996, 2004, 2007 by Tyndale House Foundation. Used by permission of Tyndale House Publishers, Inc., Carol Stream, Illinois 60188. All rights reserved.

Scripture quotations marked NASB are taken from the *New American Standard Bible*®, copyright © 1960, 1962, 1963, 1968, 1971, 1972, 1973, 1975, 1977, 1995 by The Lockman Foundation. Used by permission.

Scripture quotations marked *The Message* are taken from *The Message* by Eugene H. Peterson, copyright © 1993, 1994, 1995, 1996, 2000, 2001, 2002. Used by permission of NavPress Publishing Group. All rights reserved.

Scripture quotations marked NKJV are taken from the New King James Version®. Copyright © 1982 by Thomas Nelson, Inc. Used by permission. All rights reserved. *NKJV* is a trademark of Thomas Nelson, Inc.

Scripture quotations marked KJV are taken from the *The Holy Bible,* King James Version.

Library of Congress Cataloging-in-Publication Data to come

Carlson, Randy, date.
    The power of one thing : how to intentionally change your life / Randy Carlson.
      p. cm.
    Includes bibliographical references (p.   ).
    ISBN 978-0-8423-8222-9 (sc)
    1. Success—Religious aspects—Christianity. 2. Goal (Psychology)—Religious aspects—Christianity. I. Title.
    BV4598.3.C37 2009
    248.8′6—dc22
                                       2009022887

Printed in the United States of America

15 14 13 12 11 10 09
7   6   5   4   3   2   1

To Donna, Evan, Kelly, Andrea, Derek, and Kylie—
you motivate me to live an intentional life in Christ

CONTENTS

ACKNOWLEDGMENTS

The Power of One Thing is the result of my personal passion to help people experience the freedom and peace I've witnessed in those who have decided to live an intentional life in Christ.

This entire project evolved because of the dedication and hard work of a team of people who joined me in the passion to communicate the message in the power of one thing. First, I want to thank Barb Kois for her dedication in pulling together all my teachings on this topic, and then assisting me in shaping them into the book you hold in your hands. She spent untold hours helping to craft the final manuscript. I also want to express my appreciation to the entire Tyndale House team for catching the vision for what the power of one thing can do in a person's life and then joining me in this project. Jan Long Harris, Sharon Leavitt, Kim Miller, Sarah Atkinson, Yolanda Sidney, along with many others at Tyndale, have patiently assisted in turning an idea into reality—one word at a time.

I also want to extend much appreciation to my Intentional Living ministry team for their support and encouragement while I worked on this book. Much thanks is extended to Dawn Heitger, Steven Davis, and Shanna Gregor for providing their editorial feedback and encouragement.

I'm grateful to my radio listeners for providing the motivation for this book. I've witnessed in them the power of one thing at work. Each story in this book is a composite of what I've heard from all these dedicated listeners over the last several years. In any case where an actual story was used, we took care to protect the identity of the people who gave permission for their stories to be told.

Finally, this book would never have been possible without the loving support and encouragement of my wife, Donna. Her willingness to allow me to take time away from home in order to work on this project, not to mention her willingness to read and provide feedback on the manuscript, has been invaluable. My love for her never fades!

INTRODUCTION
What Difference Does One Thing Make?

Juliana was overwhelmed, unsure what to do next. She and her husband, Al, were the caretakers of their three young grandchildren. Their daughter, Amisha, had been in and out of drug rehab programs for more than two years. Every time she tried to take her children back to live with her, she managed for about three weeks before relapsing.

Juliana and Al had been looking forward to retirement in two years, but now the expenses of caring for their grandchildren had delayed that plan. Making matters worse, Al had atrial fibrillation, a heart condition that was aggravated by stress. The couple also had a son in the military who had been in a war zone for four months. They watched the news frantically each evening, praying his area hadn't been hit.

On top of these major stressors, Juliana was faced with the daily pressures of caring for small children again. When she called my radio program, her youngest grandchild was sick with an ear infection, his third in the last twelve months.

"I love my grandchildren and I love my daughter, but I don't know how much longer Al and I can do this," she said. "I'm so tired, and my husband isn't healthy. I don't know where to turn."

Perhaps you haven't experienced the stress of raising grandchildren, but like me, I bet you have been overwhelmed when setting out to undertake a big project or when faced with a growing list of responsibilities at work or home. *How on earth am I going to be able to do all this?* you ask yourself. Perhaps you've struggled for years to overcome a bad habit. You may even have licked it for a while, only to relapse. *How will I ever overcome this temptation for good?* you wonder.

Over the years, I've learned that intentional living is the only way out. Either you let circumstances control you or you take responsibility for what's under your control. You may not be able to make big life changes overnight, but by committing to follow through on one small thing every day, you can inch yourself closer and closer to your goal. There are many ways to fail in life, but the only way to succeed is to be intentional.

Often when people are overwhelmed, they freeze, feeling trapped and unable to move forward. My focus when talking with Juliana, then, was to get her to identify her biggest source of stress. We could then identify the "one thing" that would bring her the greatest relief. Clearly, her biggest stressor was her relationship with Amisha. Specifically, Juliana said she was tired of trying to motivate her daughter to make positive changes, only to be let down again and again.

Juliana explained that Amisha often missed her counseling appointments and supervised visits with the kids. Every time Juliana reminded her of the importance of these meetings, Amisha offered excuse after excuse about why she'd missed another appointment. Usually, the two ended up arguing, which compounded the stress Juliana was feeling. No wonder she felt paralyzed by her situation. After all, she had no control over Amisha's decisions.

There are many ways to fail in life, but the only way to succeed is to be intentional.

These fruitless confrontations were causing Juliana great stress, but she could put herself back in control by changing her communication pattern with her daughter. Instead of trying to reason with Amisha when she offered another excuse, Juliana might simply say, "I need to go now. I'll talk to you later" before hanging up. It might feel uncomfortable and make her daughter mad, but that one small change could alter the dynamic in their conversations and prevent Juliana from feeling unproductive frustration.

You'll notice I didn't offer Juliana a profound solution or even ten steps she could take to remedy her situation. Once she realized that she wasn't really stuck, that she could move forward simply by becoming intentional about addressing what was in her control—one small step at a time—Juliana knew she'd found a way to move beyond her anxiety and find renewed hope.

In my life, my counseling practice, and my radio ministry, I have discovered that one reason people don't make progress toward their goals is that they get overwhelmed with the enormity of the task. They might have done things the same way for ten, twenty, forty, or more years, and doing things differently and better seems impossible.

Yet I've learned that by taking a step-by-step approach that breaks down the journey from here to there into doable chunks, I can get there. I can do one small thing today that will improve all my tomorrows. The same is true for you. Doing just one small thing will give you a feeling of accomplishment and hope that you will be able to keep taking action to improve your situation.

I'm convinced that doing one thing each day, as Juliana did—just one small but important thing—can change your life.

NOT A TYPICAL GOAL-SETTING BOOK

It sounds so simple, doesn't it? Perhaps you've heard about goal setting on the job or read about it in a book. Countless articles and books, talk shows, Web sites, blogs, and motivational programs offer great advice about achieving your goals. Experts always tell you to make a list of action steps to take you where you want to go. It's good advice. So why do so few people actually follow through on something so basic?

First, multiple-step programs or complicated lists of rules and procedures simply overwhelm us. And as Juliana discovered, no one can make multiple changes at once. She needed to change one thing within her control—how she responded to Amisha—and practice it until it became a habit.

Second, change takes effort; inertia takes none. Once our initial enthusiasm wears off, we have little incentive to keep working toward our goals—especially when we don't see results as quickly as we'd like. Like most parents, Juliana wanted to support and protect her daughter, so stepping back didn't feel easy or natural at first.

What we need is a simple yet effective way to take actions that will get us where we want to go. Gaining on our goals must be done incrementally, little by little, one step at a time. That's actually good news; it means that if we are willing to do just one thing toward one goal today, we will be on our way to a better life.

Think of the steady dripping of water that helped to shape the Grand Canyon—or the loose change you toss into a jar that builds up to a large sum over time. Small things, done over time, yield big results.

GETTING THE MOST FROM THIS BOOK

In part 1 of this book, we'll look more closely at the power of one thing and the factors that prevent so many individuals from mastering this strategy. We'll also examine the link between intentionality and the power of one thing. Then I'll help you determine which one or two "one things" will make the biggest payoff in your life.

One reason people don't make progress toward their goals is that they get overwhelmed with the enormity of the task.

In part 2, I'll get more specific about practical ways to improve your life one step at a time. As I've counseled others, I have discovered nine personal challenges that get in the way of living a fulfilling life (see the italicized words in the list below). When someone describes a life struggle to me, the issue can almost always be traced back to one of these areas.

And meaningful change begins when the person makes one small change in a problem area. In this second section, you'll be able to consider these nine issues more closely and discover how you can harness the power of one thing done in the area(s) that will improve your life most significantly:

The power of one thing will change your *thinking*.
The power of one thing will change your *attitude*.
The power of one thing will change your *emotions*.
The power of one thing will change your *words*.
The power of one thing will change *how you use your time*.
The power of one thing will change *how you pick friends*.
The power of one thing will *unclutter your life*.
The power of one thing will change *the questions you ask*.
The power of one thing will change *how you make decisions*.

By identifying the root of your underlying struggle, you can determine the one thing that will begin to turn your life around.

Notice that the first three areas in the list above are related to the mind. That's where it all starts—everything flows from our thought life. Matthew 12:34 says, "Out of the overflow of the heart the mouth speaks."

We will examine the power of one thing to change your thinking, your attitude, and your emotions.

Once you are thinking properly, you can tackle some unhealthy behaviors. After all, right thinking shows up in right actions, the next four areas we'll look at. We'll see how the power of one thing can change your words, your use of time, and your choice of friends, and even clear the clutter in your surroundings and in your life.

Toward the end of the book, we'll look at two final areas, and you'll see how the work you have done to that point will give you the wisdom to ask better questions and make better decisions.

So what's the best way to work through the book? By the time you finish reading part 1, you may have identified the area that is your biggest challenge. If so, you may choose to turn to the chapter in part 2 that focuses on that topic. Each chapter explains why that area is a make-it-or-break-it part of life and offers numerous ideas of how to improve it—along with some ideas of the one thing you might do to initiate positive change. You can certainly adopt or modify one of these or select another "one thing" altogether. Once you've made that first "one thing" a habit, you might begin to focus on yet another step.

While you probably will get the most payoff from addressing the area at the root of your greatest struggle, you can also take your life up a notch simply by making one or more small changes in each of the other areas as well.

If, even after reading part 1, you're not sure where you'd like to make that first small change, I suggest you read part 2 in order, from chapter 5 through chapter 14. At some point, you're likely to think, *That's it—one small change here could put me on the path to a better life!*

Whichever way you choose to work through the book, I firmly believe that the power of one thing will work for you . . . that one thing done intentionally over time will improve your life.

Let's get started.

PART ONE

You Are Only "One Thing" Away from a Better Life

1

DO ONE SMALL THING—INTENTIONALLY

The person who knows one thing and does it better than anyone else, even if it only be the art of raising lentils, receives the crown he merits.

—AUGUSTINE "OG" MANDINO,
TWENTIETH-CENTURY MOTIVATIONAL TEACHER

Whoever or whatever is most intentional in your life wins—the difference between winners and losers comes down to this profound truth. What do I mean by *intentional*? I use it to describe the driving force in an area of your life—physical health, let's say. A woman who is more intentional about shedding ten pounds than sleeping later each morning might begin setting the alarm for an earlier time so she can hit the treadmill for twenty minutes. By following through on one small thing—an early-morning walk—it is clear that she values physical fitness above extra sleep. To make any positive change in your life, you must create an action plan and summon the determination to intentionally get to your goal, one small step at a time.

Notice I say successful people are *intentional*, not merely *well intentioned*. The key is commitment plus action. We can have great ideas about what we want to do next, but if we are not committed to actually changing what we do and how we think, nothing much will change. In Luke 18:18-22 (NLT), we read,

> Once a religious leader asked Jesus this question: "Good Teacher, what should I do to inherit eternal life?"
>
> "Why do you call me good?" Jesus asked him. "Only God

is truly good. But to answer your question, you know the commandments: 'You must not commit adultery. You must not murder. You must not steal. You must not testify falsely. Honor your father and mother.'"

The man replied, "I've obeyed all these commandments since I was young."

When Jesus heard his answer, he said, "There is still one thing you haven't done. Sell all your possessions and give the money to the poor, and you will have treasure in heaven. Then come, follow me."

Jesus was talking about commitment plus action. He knew that the man's wealth and position stood in the way of his total commitment. Although the man had the desire to do the right thing, he was not fully committed and lacked the willingness to act. As a result, he passed up the opportunity to follow Christ wholeheartedly. His life was not transformed.

> *Whoever or whatever is most intentional in your life wins.*

You need to recognize that something drives everything you do. The rich ruler was driven by his possessions and status. You have only two choices—either you become the most intentional force in your life or you allow someone or something else to exert more influence over your life. If you're not the most intentional about yourself, someone or something else will be—that's a promise. You might know people who would love to run your life . . . or substances waiting to run your life . . . or emotions that are ready to run your life. You decide—who or what is going to win today?

If you're like me, you want to succeed at what is most important to you, but you sometimes find it challenging to stay focused on your top priorities. Your good intentions don't translate into the accomplishment of worthy goals. Some days everything seems to be trying to sabotage your efforts. Distractions come at you from all directions, and your time is probably eaten up by demands every hour of the day.

You can be your own worst saboteur as well. Procrastination, laziness, discouragement, and disorganization strike everyone at some point. You may be skilled at multitasking, which can actually make you feel on top of your game when you are anything but. When you're driving and talking on your cell phone, neither the person you're talking to nor your fellow drivers are getting your best. Recently I heard a radio broadcast in which listeners were told that the brain can't really focus on more than one task at once.[1] Conse-

If you're not the most intentional about yourself, someone or something else will be—that's a promise.

quently, when you multitask, your brain shifts quickly from one activity to another rather than focusing at least a little on each of the several things you're doing.

FROM INTENTION TO ACTION

As you've seen, having good intentions is easy. Being intentional—making an effort to reach important goals—is difficult. But it's not impossible.

Intentionality is critical; without it, you would never be motivated to change. But following through on your intentions is often manageable only when you focus on the next one thing you need to do to bring about change.

I tend to go off in numerous directions at once. I have lots of interests, lots of questions, lots of projects, lots of what-ifs. If you're at all like me, you can end up on lots of rabbit trails guided by your good intentions. And, as we know, the road to you-know-where is paved with good intentions. So what I'm about to show you comes from my own journey of moving beyond good intentions to life-changing results.

For me, getting focused happened when I was hit with one of those difficult, life-altering events. When my mother died in August 2005, eleven years after my dad, I suddenly realized I was an adult orphan. I was now part of the oldest generation in our family, and the shortness of life came into clear focus. Like the psalmist, my prayer became "Teach me to number my days" (see Psalm 90:12). I knew that if I was to turn my good intentions into reality, I needed to change the way I used my time and resources and start using the power of one thing to change my own life.

I wanted my life to count, and I became focused on my legacy. My parents had lived with integrity and commitment, and they ended strong. I wanted the same for myself. My parents had given up a big house in the suburbs and my dad's high-paying job in order to follow a dream . . . to build a ranch where disadvantaged children could get away from their dysfunctional situations for a while.

I realized that my tendency to overcommit, which sometimes led to procrastination, could keep me from living with a similar sense of purpose. I decided that the only way to finish life strong would be to break the rest of my life into bite-size commitments—one thing done each day in one or more essential areas of life. I realized that my legacy would be the accumulation of a series of "one things" lived out over an extended period of time—the rest of my life. I'm so committed to the power of one thing that I created a One Thing wristband that I wear every day as a reminder to do the one thing that day that will make the biggest difference in my life. Others have asked me about my wristband, and now thousands wear one just like it.[2]

A Lesson from Tiger Woods

Every big accomplishment is preceded by lots of little, seemingly insignificant actions—resulting in the one big thing everyone sees. The other day, I watched as Tiger Woods won another PGA tournament on national television, but what the audience never saw was the hundreds of hours when Tiger, all alone, worked on perfecting his swing—one practice swing after another—far from the eyes of the public.

While Woods is a dramatic example, we see the same principle in all areas of life. We cheer when our son or daughter wins a statewide musical competition, but we don't have film footage of the hours the child spent practicing alone in his or her room. We congratulate a married couple on the accomplishment of a fifty-year marriage, but we weren't around to witness how they stuck together one day . . . one challenge . . . one disagreement . . . one illness at a time over those fifty years.

To illustrate how the power of one thing can lead to big accomplishments in your own life, try this exercise. Take a piece of paper and draw a horizontal line across the top. On the left side, write the year of your birth, and on the right side, write this year. In between, mark off the paper in five- or ten-year increments to make your time line. On your time line mark the major events, accomplishments, and changes next to the year they occurred. For example:

when you met Christ
when you went to college
when you got married
when you solved a major problem
when a child was born
when you made a decision to go in a new direction in your life
when you started a business
when you paid off your house
loss of a child
loss of a job
major health crisis

Most people can list about a dozen "big things" in their lives. Once you have written them down, think about the questions below:

- What small things preceded and followed each event? List all the "one things" that led up to that one big thing. Were they a series of interactions, a series of choices and behaviors, or people you associated with?
- What pattern do you see? Are the significant events largely positive? Are they growth oriented? Or are they largely negative events that caused you pain? What does this indicate about how intentional you are? Who or what was most intentional leading up to each big thing?
- How has your life changed as a result of each event?

Now extend your time line into the future. What is the next significant thing you are hoping for in the future? Are you working toward something that will result in a positive "big thing" in your life? Or are you just letting things happen? Your future will become reality only if today you remain focused on the most important next one thing.

For example, if the next important stop on your time line is to successfully raise your teenage daughter, then it is essential that you have a game plan to make that goal a reality. Start by making a list of all the "one things" you can think of that will be required of you to raise your daughter well.

- I need to deal with a bad attitude about my ex-spouse, my daughter's father.
- I need to establish expectations and routines for myself.
- I need to pray for my daughter daily.
- I need to be more confident when I make a decision and not give in so easily to her demands.
- I need to hold my daughter accountable for her actions and not respond out of guilt.
- I need to monitor her relationships and get to know her friends better.
- I need to encourage her strengths.
- I need to stop criticizing her so much.

Your future will become reality only if today you remain focused on the most important next one thing.

Even though the list may get long and feel pretty overwhelming to you, the power of doing the next right one thing is the only path to success. Remember, healthy change will occur only when the power of one thing is used. By doing the first right one thing followed by the next one thing until each is completed or has become a habit, you almost guarantee yourself success in what matters most.

When I look across my time line, I identify the following as the most significant moments in my adult life: my marriage to Donna, the birth of our children, the decision we made to move from Michigan to Arizona, the decision I made to finish my graduate work and go on for a doctorate, my decision in 1988 to write my first book, and the decision in 1990 to start a radio program to help families. I realize that each of these big moments represents a move or a change, something new. But each of these events in my life was preceded by many small "one things."

WHY ONE THING REALLY DOES MAKE A DIFFERENCE

We can only really live today one thing at a time—one thought, one idea, one relationship, one phone call at a time. Matthew 6:34 (NLT) tells us, "Don't worry about tomorrow, for tomorrow will bring its own worries. Today's trouble is enough for today." We can't rush ahead; we can't lag behind. So how does change happen? Think of it this way:

> One thing done once is an experience.
> One thing done twice has your attention.
> One thing done often is a pursuit.
> One thing done always is a habit.

It has been said that our choices become our habits and our habits become our character. Our choices add up and determine the overall quality of our lives.

As you learn to choose one small change and focus on it one day at a time, your life is going to get better. After you have made the first thing a habit and experienced the satisfaction of having achieved a small but significant milestone, you can tackle one more thing with energy and confidence.

By doing the first right one thing followed by the next one thing until each is completed or has become a habit, you almost guarantee yourself success in what matters most.

I've seen it happen—in my own life and in the lives of others—doing just one thing differently can produce significant and lasting changes for the better.

The key is how you manage each of the "one things" you do each day—the tasks, conversations, relationships, and projects that make up your life. Remember the advice of Solomon: "Go to the ant, you sluggard; consider its ways and be wise!" (Proverbs 6:6). Ants are commonly thought of as industrious creatures. Ever noticed how ab-solutely focused they appear as they head back to their colonies, haul-ing crumbs several times bigger than themselves?

Our choices become our habits and our habits become our character.

In this proverb, Solomon urges un-motivated individuals to follow the ant's example. He knew that people who do one thing intentionally over an extended period of time can change their lives. Don't be discouraged by how far you think you need to go. Instead, be encouraged as you consider the following:

Doing one thing to intentionally love your spouse each day will change your marriage.

Doing one thing to intentionally read God's Word and pray each day for even a few minutes will lead to spiritual growth in your life.

Doing one thing to exercise each day will lead to better physical health.

Doing one thing to be truthful and reliable each day will result in people counting on you.

Doing one thing to control your anger each day will reduce violence, abuse, and the likelihood of divorce in your home.

Doing one thing to maintain healthy opposite-sex friendships each day will prevent the destructive results from emotional or physical affairs.

Once you begin linking a number of these one small things—like pearls on a chain, each representing one small, positive change—you eventually will have a long, solid chain of improvements.

Warning: The power of one thing can be your friend or your enemy. Un-fortunately, a string of negative actions also accumulates. If you ignore the signs and symptoms of poor health, for example, eventually you might find that you have a serious and advanced illness. If month after month you spend a little more money than you earn, you can wind up in serious financial trouble. If you don't discipline your child during the early years because he or she is just so cute, you are likely to raise a brat.

Warning: The power of one thing can be your friend or your enemy.

One small action leads to another, and they join together, for good or ill. Perhaps you have determined to improve your life before. As you probably discovered, it's far easier to slip back into destructive patterns than to achieve positive and lasting change. After all, when we do nothing, our situation just naturally deteriorates; improvement takes intentionality and consistent action. If you have tried to change before, only to give up, keep reading. The next chapter was written just for you.

2

"BUT I'VE TRIED TO CHANGE BEFORE. . . ."

To exist is to change, to change is to mature, to mature is to go on creating oneself endlessly.

—HENRI BERGSON, NINETEENTH-CENTURY
FRENCH PHILOSOPHER

I remember the day I decided to put away my saxophone for good. Until that day, I'd enjoyed playing a musical instrument and thought I was pretty good. In fact, my dad, my brother, and I used to play together as the Carlson Trio. In earlier years, my dad had been a professional saxophonist, and my brother Larry is accomplished on the keyboard. We even recorded two albums together.

I completely abandoned the saxophone in the office of Northwest High School when I registered as a new transfer junior from out of state. The school secretary had sounded excited when she heard I played an instrument. Apparently the band needed some help, so she immediately phoned the band instructor, asking him to come down and meet the incoming musical prodigy.

After a brief welcome, the instructor, whose name I long ago repressed, asked what instrument I played. I told him I played the alto saxophone. His look said it all, but he decided to say it anyway: "Oh, great, all I need is another saxophone player." Then he turned and walked out of the office.

From stubbornness, I suppose, I didn't join his band and never even entered the band room. That was a mistake! I allowed this insensitive band instructor to be more intentional about my music than I was. I violated the first rule of intentional living: be more intentional about yourself than anyone else is.

When you decide to live differently, your mind will naturally start coming up with excuses—often the result of discouraging past experiences—to tell you why you can't or shouldn't do it. Perhaps you have already come up with your list of reasons why you can't really change:

> I don't have time.
> I've failed at this before.
> I'm not as good as my sister.
> It never works out for me anyway.
> I don't know how.
> I don't have the willpower.
> I've been doing it this way for twenty years.
> Everyone in my family does it that way.
> I can't do it because of the stress in my job.
> I can't do it because of the stress in my family.
> I can't do it because of my health limitations.
> I can't do it because of my financial limitations.

You get the picture—there are innumerable excuses why you "can't" do something and only one really great reason why you can. You can do one important thing today because God said you can. Philippians 4:13 (NLT) says, "I can do everything through Christ, who gives me strength." Ultimately the power of one thing to change your life comes from the power of God to change your life.

THE ENEMIES OF CHANGE

The key to success is commitment plus action. You can have great ideas of what you want to do, but if excuses keep you from acting, nothing much will change. Just as a band teacher's insensitive remarks derailed my future as a saxophonist, so many things can keep each of us from positive change. Let's take a closer look at some of them.

Discouragement, the enemy of change

When parents feel like failures, I've noticed they generally try to make up for it with their own strength—a father gets tougher on his children or a mother gives up and withdraws. One of my favorite parenting verses is Ecclesiastes 9:17: "The quiet words of the wise are more to be heeded than the shouts of a ruler of fools." We parents don't have to be stronger or louder or more intense to be effective. We must be wise and intentional, or deliberate, in the way we lead our children.

I've witnessed business leaders over the years make absolutely stupid decisions that ultimately led to personal and business ruin. Most often, they got off track during times of high stress. They felt insecure in their leadership ability and exerted their personal power or persuasiveness to compensate.

Here are the seven steps to discouragement:

Step 1: I need to change.
Step 2: I want to change.
Step 3: I commit to change.
Step 4: I try to change.
Step 5: I meet resistance to change.
Step 6: I stop changing and go back to what I was doing before.
Step 7: I feel discouraged because I didn't change and my
        commitment is gone—until I start the cycle all over again.

An effective, successful parent or businessperson needs to be intentional and confident about assuming his or her rightful leadership role, understanding that resistance to doing the right thing is normal and to be expected. You can be intentional in your family, your work, or your church even if the people around you or your circumstances don't change. Become a different person yourself, and as you grow, everything around you will appear to be changing too.

Commitment takes hard work—whether it's a commitment to your marriage, a career, or a lifelong dream. Doing one thing to improve your life is going to take work. It means rising above the discouragement that you may feel if you face a setback or if change seems to be coming too slowly. But the beauty of God's plan is that he promises to give you the strength to accomplish good things if you are committed—really committed—to him. He doesn't leave you out there on your own to accomplish Herculean tasks.

Anxiety, the enemy of change

You may be feeling a little anxious right now, remembering times you set out to change your life, only to fail. It's easier to allow negative changes to creep into your life than it is to accomplish positive changes. It takes little or no effort for your eating habits to slip from healthy to unhealthy. All it takes is a couple of extra stops for fast food when you're too rushed to cook dinner at home. Eating only healthy meals, on the other hand, takes work.

One lesson I began learning in graduate school was that anxiety is always produced by looking backward or forward. One of my professors put it this way: "The further we move either back in time or ahead in time from this very moment, the more anxious and out of control we feel." The past is over, and only God knows what is going to happen tomorrow—and you have no control over that either. So you must live for today, intentionally doing the one small thing that will take you another step closer to your goal.

I know that's easier said than done, but once again, God comes through for us with a verse that is perfect to latch onto by reading or memorization. We can recite it while breathing deeply to combat anxiety: "Be anxious for nothing, but in everything by prayer and supplication, with thanksgiving, let your requests be made known to God; and the peace of God, which surpasses all understanding, will guard your hearts and minds through Christ Jesus" (Philippians 4:6-7, NKJV).

The further we move either back in time or ahead in time, the more anxious and out of control we feel.

The out-of-your-control issues are in God's very capable hands, where you must leave them, trusting his promises to work good out of even evil events and circumstances. In the meantime, you choose to be angry or kind; to exercise or watch TV; to use encouraging words or hurtful ones; to give in to an addiction or, by God's grace, use self-control to avoid such a trap.

And each day, you can make the choice to begin again. As the apostle Paul says, "One thing I do: Forgetting what is behind and straining toward what is ahead, I press on toward the goal" (Philippians 3:13-14).

Will you join Paul and me in putting the past behind you and straining toward a better future by concentrating on just one thing? If so, you are embarking on an intentional life, and you will be glad you did.

The intentional life must be lived one moment at a time, one thing at a time. Living in the past or the future can create anxiety. Christ-centeredness means living this moment in him.

Disruptions, the enemy of change

Lynn began an exercise program on New Year's Day. Getting up early to go to the health club or stopping there on her way home from work was often a struggle. But she was determined to go three times a week to improve her health, her mental attitude, and her weight.

By March, she was in the habit of going three times a week. Even when she was out of town for business or a vacation, she dutifully found a place to use a treadmill, StairMaster, or stationary bike so she could continue what she hoped was becoming a habit.

In June, after Lynn's mother was diagnosed with a serious illness, Lynn spent every spare minute helping her and accompanying her to doctor's appointments. She still wanted to exercise, but the first few weeks after her mother's diagnosis, Lynn made it to the health club only two times a week. One week she made it only once.

Lynn was disappointed that her good habit was being crowded out by this health emergency, but she didn't know what to do. When she got home after visiting her mother, she was exhausted and needed to go to bed so she could get up for work the next morning.

By September her mother's health had improved, so she no longer needed frequent doctor appointments. Lynn visited only on weekends to help her buy groceries and prepare meals for the week.

It had now been a couple of months since Lynn had exercised regularly. But she could get right back to her three-times-a-week pattern, right? That didn't happen. It was a lot easier to slip back into inactivity than it had been to establish a new, positive habit. Once Lynn's schedule became crowded, exercise slipped in priority, and her good habit disappeared.

Lynn's experience is a reminder that unexpected events—whether an illness, an accident, or a child's bad decision—do happen. Sometimes even minor disruptions at home or work will get you off track as you pursue the one thing you've determined to do to improve your life. You can't control everything in life, but in this book I want to focus on those you can, including your thoughts, attitudes, and behaviors.

You see, you—like Lynn—have more power than you think. Yes, starting an exercise regimen again would be difficult for Lynn. Essentially, she would have to start from scratch. Yet the decision to make time for the gym again was totally within her control. The power of one thing to change your life will involve times when you feel like a failure, but you can hold yourself accountable by simply picking yourself back up and once again doing the next right one thing.

Waiting, the enemy of change

I don't know about you, but waiting drives me crazy! Waiting for my waistline to shrink, waiting for the person ahead of me in line, waiting for a vacation, waiting for good health, waiting for a good marriage, waiting to grow spiritually, even waiting for Christmas—we all have to wait. Have you ever noticed that it seems to take more time when you are waiting for something good than when you are waiting for something bad? Waiting for a birthday, Christmas, a loved one, the love of your life, or a promotion seems to take forever. Trying to rush into success is like trying to rush into love—you may think you are there before you really are.

Vince Lombardi said the "dictionary is the only place that success comes before work. Hard work is the price that you must pay for success. I think you can accomplish anything if you are willing to pay the price."

Are you willing to pay the price? I can promise you that your hard work will pay off. Furthermore, the power of doing one small thing is that even a relatively simple change, done day after day, will produce results you can see fairly quickly.

SURVIVAL VERSUS SIGNIFICANCE

I've been a counselor, coach, and consultant for twenty-five years. During that time I helped patch up a lot of people and get them back into the game of life. Too many of them fell right back into the same old hole.

As a result, I was a frustrated people helper. Then, a couple of years ago, I decided that I would give the rest of my days to helping people who are committed and intentional about pursuing life at a higher level. Those who succeed and move on with their lives are those who consciously decide to grow, change, and head in a healthy new direction. They are committed to and intentional about making their lives better. I'm not talking about perfection, which cannot be attained here on earth. But today I look for people who are committed to pursuing an intentional life in Christ. If that's your desire too, I am convinced you can succeed. As an Intentional Living coach, I am passionate about helping you turn your good intentions into reality.

Most people spend their days trying to simply survive—survive at work to get a promotion and a bigger paycheck and put more into their pension plan so they can retire. Or survive in marriage without ever expecting to give or receive the deep, abiding love that every couple should experience. Or survive in raising their kids until they grow up and leave the house.

In survival mode we focus on three things. First, we focus on perfection—keeping it together for appearance's sake. This is really a form of control. When we act like perfectionists, we are frustrated by our quest to be perfect. We're concerned about what other people think. Second, in survival mode we hold on tightly to things—whether people, jobs, or rules—because they give us meaning. We stick around people who help us feel better about ourselves, or we stay in a job because it has a title or a paycheck. Third, we start to identify with what we own—a home, a car, a boat—and then want more things to help us feel more secure.

It's my passion to help you turn your good intentions into reality.

The goal of intentional living is to move from survival to significance. In significance mode, you focus on managing risk as best you can. Yet you do so, not to look good on the outside, but to keep from being distracted from your goal. Second, you are sold out to a purpose, a plan, or a passion, not to things. Your title, job, spouse, home, or possessions aren't what give you significance. In fact, your goal is simplicity, which allows you to focus on your priorities. You are willing to give things away and help others. C. S. Lewis captured the wisdom of this approach when he said, "Nothing that you have not given away will be really yours."[3]

In the next two chapters, we'll consider how to decide which one small thing will get you on the road to significance. After all, you must be intentional and choose how you live; otherwise, simply by default, life will choose for you. I know I don't want to live that kind of random, unfocused life. Do you?

3
READY . . . SET . . . KNOW!

Let us not look back in anger or forward in fear, but around in awareness.

—JAMES THURBER, AUTHOR

One day when I was working in my home office, our German shepherd, Sandy, came in, sat down, and stared at the full-length mirror on the wall behind me. It was obvious that she was completely unaware of herself in the mirror—no recognition at all. I was amazed that she could look into that mirror and show no evidence of seeing her own image. It was as though the mirror weren't even there and she was staring at a blank wall. Then it dawned on me that many times we humans are not all that different. We go through our days doing many things without ever being fully aware of why or what difference they're really going to make anyway. Like Sandy, we look but we don't see.

As you begin to think about the greatest challenge in your own life, how can you be sure you identify the one thing you need to do to turn the situa-

We look but we don't see.

tion around? One key is to become more self-aware. Otherwise, like Sandy, you may be oblivious to what's right in front of you—or more to the point, right inside you.

KNOWING YOURSELF
You might argue that, in our culture, we are often all too aware of ourselves—what we want, what we need, what we don't have, what others

21

think of us, and on and on. Self-centered egotism isn't what I'm recommending; instead, I'm encouraging you to become increasingly self-aware. Knowing how you're wired and pinpointing your blind spots can help you identify the one thing that will jump-start positive change in your life. For instance, I'm aware of my tendency to take on too many projects at once, and I've used that awareness about myself to intentionally stay focused on the most important things.

Know how you're wired

You won't know what one thing to tackle first—in fact, you won't even know what area of your life most needs attention—until you have accurate self-awareness. One woman I talked to had recently struggled to sort out her work projects. She created lists and Excel spreadsheets to try to get organized. Finally, in desperation, she approached her manager and said, "I'm really floundering in my work. I can't seem to get it organized and sorted into doable portions. Could I show you what I'm up against and talk to you about it?"

The manager gladly agreed. This woman then spent about twenty minutes explaining the problem to her manager as he asked questions, made comments, and nodded his head at appropriate times. Then the employee stopped and said, "Suddenly it's clear how I should proceed. I learned years ago that it really helps me to talk things through with someone, but I had forgotten that. I've been trying to figure it out by myself, and I've been getting deeper and deeper into a hole." The one small thing she may choose to begin doing to keep herself on track is to schedule a standing weekly appointment with her boss to talk through her workload.

You won't know what one thing to tackle first until you have accurate self-awareness.

Personality tests, strengths tests, and career aptitude tests—today's students take many more self-assessment and diagnostic tools than they did when I was in school. Many businesses make such tools part of their hiring or team-building process as well. Fortunately, if you haven't had the opportunity to take such an assessment at school or work, dozens of excellent diagnostic tools are also available in books and online to help you assess your personality style, learning style, areas of strength, and more. After you get the results, talk to your spouse, a friend, or a supervisor about the results and see if what you learned about yourself rings true to him or her.

Understanding how you solve problems, how you learn, how you prefer to be acknowledged or recognized for a job well done, what activities are energizing or exhausting to you, what motivates you to keep on in a new habit, or whether you prefer to relate to people in groups or individually—these insights will make you more successful because you will know what works for you.

Know your blind spots

Being aware of yourself also means recognizing your blind spots and vulnerabilities. We all have them—areas that make us less effective because we're not even aware we're stuck there. Do you have someone who can help you with your blind spots by offering you loving, constructive feedback (not harsh criticism)?

My wife, Donna, knows where my blind spots are and I know where hers are, so we make a great team. I wish I'd paid more attention to her gentle warnings recently when I was feeling overwhelmed. Not only was I on deadline to complete this book, I also needed to prepare lessons for our radio program, plan an upcoming retreat for our board of directors, and help our daughter prepare for a mission trip. I was also determined to finish landscaping our yard.

I finally arranged to take a week off to concentrate on these projects. I decided to tackle the yard work first, figuring that once I got that out of the way, I could concentrate on more important things. Here in Tucson many of us landscape our yards with rocks, since it's so expensive and difficult to maintain a lawn in the heat. I had the project finished in my mind before I even started, with all the rocks exactly where I wanted them. I figured I could finish the job in no more than fifteen to twenty hours.

I was very intentional in laying out the design; I was intentional in ordering twenty tons of rock, which were delivered right on schedule. I was intentional in setting aside the time, and I was intentional about reminding my wife that I could do this without anybody's help. The rocks would need to be moved and laid by hand, and I figured I could move the rocks at the rate of a ton an hour. I was sure I'd be finished in no more than twenty hours max. I was intentional all right, but I was soon to discover that I was wrong about almost all my estimates and too proud to admit it to my patient and observant wife.

As I was getting ready to begin this job, Donna asked, "Randy, why don't you find a couple of high school or college students who are looking to earn a few extra bucks to come help you?"

Like so many guys, I resisted the suggestion that I needed help. I told her, "No way! I can do this. I know exactly how I want to do it." (I didn't mention that I was also too cheap to hire anybody.)

Thirty-two hours into the project I still had ten tons of rock to lay. I was exhausted, sunburned, and ornery. My week off was flying by. Donna didn't say much—she backed off and just gave me a little smile now and then. Finally, on the last day of my week off, I broke down and hired three young men (one was the kid who delivered our pizza), and they came and helped me finish the job.

While I had been very intentional about this project, I had been unintentionally wrong! I would have been much smarter to listen to my wife. If I had, I would have noticed that she was pointing out a blind spot: my tendency to take on too much. I lost four days of my life (vacation time, no less!) that I could have used on much more important tasks if I had just listened to Donna's counsel. So you see, you're not alone in wandering from the path of living intentionally smart from day to day.

KNOWING OTHERS

Too often when we want to change our lives for the better, we focus first on the problems we think others are causing us. But focusing on one thing that will fix someone else or shifting the blame to another person or situation won't work. That doesn't mean we shouldn't try to understand other people, but we do need to recognize that only we can make our own lives better.

The world around you starts with the small world you live in—the people you interact with on a daily basis. If you have a spouse and children, are you aware of their thoughts, dreams, hurts, needs, and aspirations? Do you regularly talk with each of your family members, focusing intently on being quiet and simply listening and really hearing what each has to say? Or are you so busy planning your next statement or thinking about what you need to do as soon as you finish the conversation that you aren't really connecting with or learning about the person's thoughts and feelings? You're there but you're not aware.

Focusing on one thing that will fix someone else won't work.

Once you understand the needs of your wife, husband, or children, you can better identify an area in your life that you want to work on. If your children cringe when you start in on your regular lecture or if they seem afraid to share their thoughts with you, perhaps you'll decide that the first "one thing" you need to do pertains to your attitude.

Once you are in tune with those you live with, your circle can grow. If you're discouraged because you're floundering on the job or unable to build meaningful relationships in your neighborhood or church, begin considering what one small thing you can do to begin resolving the situation. Then start doing that one thing today.

Being a keen observer of the people in your life can also help you see how others perceive you. Their insights might help you decide what one thing you want to start on in your life. As you seek to understand others, remember to separate your issues and problems from theirs. Be sure the one thing you choose to work on is not something that only your spouse/child/friend can change.

KNOWING GOD

As you learn more about yourself and others, don't forget your deep need to know and understand God and his plans for your life. All the tests and books and counseling sessions in the world are limited because they are human efforts.

Knowing God is the most important kind of awareness you can ever attain, and it is a never-ending quest. As Isaiah 55:8-9 says, "'My thoughts are not your thoughts, neither are your ways my ways,' declares the LORD.

'As the heavens are higher than the earth, so are my ways higher than your ways and my thoughts than your thoughts.'" Yet God offers a great promise: "You will seek me and find me when you seek me with all your heart" (Jeremiah 29:13).

The best place to gain true self-awareness is in God's presence. Ask him to show you how he sees you and how you can use the insights of others to improve your life. He promises that we can find him when we seek him and that he will give us wisdom if we only ask (see James 1:5). Be quiet in his presence and wait for him to help you understand how you can honor him by working on one thing at a time in your life.

4
WHERE DO YOU WANT TO GROW FIRST?

I do not think much of a man who is not wiser today than he was yesterday.
—ABRAHAM LINCOLN

A man called our radio program and said, "I live in Montana and just lost my job. I want to move my family back to northern Ohio, where my wife's family lives. Do you think I should do this?"

He was considering a decision that, on the surface, sounded great. He'd be moving near family and gaining the day-to-day support of grandparents. But as we continued to talk, I learned there was more to the story. This man had held five jobs in six years, and he had been fired from each of them. His teenage children resented having to pick up and move each time Dad got fired. They were just starting to get established in a church and were making friends. Moving wasn't something they wanted to do.

In my Intentional Living coaching, I've discovered that people often ask the wrong questions trying to get to the right answer. They'll never find it that way. The decision about whether to move his family wasn't really the right question at all. The problem was that this man had an unstable work record and was having trouble providing for his family. He hadn't dealt with the personal problems that caused him to go through job after job. The correct question to ask would have been, "What do I need to do to become a father who can intentionally provide for my family?"

Before you start thinking about which area you want to tackle first, you need to identify the root problem or issue. If, like the caller, you work on the wrong problem—usually a surface issue covering something deeper—it will be like trying to cover a cancerous growth with a Band-Aid, hoping the cancer will go away. As we discussed in the last chapter, one way to ensure you do land on the right "one thing" is to know your own strengths and weaknesses, along with the needs of those around you.

This chapter is devoted to providing you with further help as you choose the correct "one thing" to tackle. I've included the following five intentional living steps to help you correctly identify the next big one thing that you need to work on and how you can start the process today:

1. **State the problem clearly, or you might end up working on the wrong problem.** Most people tend to want out from their current problem—now! No wonder so many try to tackle a problem without thinking through it; they take a "Ready, *fire*, aim" approach rather than a "Ready, *aim*, fire" one. To avoid making this mistake, you need to clearly identify the core problem and root issues that are standing in the way of your accomplishing the one thing that is important to you. Otherwise, you may commit to start doing one thing that won't really make a difference.

   In Genesis 4 we find a classic example of someone identifying the wrong problem. Cain and Abel brought their offerings to the Lord—Abel brought the best of his newborn lambs as a gift, and Cain brought some crops from his field. God rejected Cain's offering because it was merely a token gift, not what God had required. Cain could have looked at the situation honestly and confessed to God that he'd offered a sacrifice out of obligation rather than worship. Instead he became jealous of Abel and figured he'd solve his dilemma by killing his brother.

   By failing to identify the problem in his own heart (jealousy), Cain impulsively turned on his brother, thinking that would solve the problem. But it only made things worse. Cain would have profited from looking at the situation from another angle. That's what I encourage you to do—consider looking at your challenge from another perspective. You must first clearly and correctly state the problem before you can intentionally fix it.

If you identify the source or cause of a problem incorrectly, as Cain did, you won't be able to solve it. In fact, trying to fix or blame someone else may simply compound the situation. Because this first step is so key—and sometimes the hardest to do successfully—let's spend some time considering how to be sure you correctly identify the core issue.

a. *Make the problem clear.* When my friends and I played darts as children, we would stand way back and carefully aim for the center of the dartboard. Most of the time our shots would stick in wallboard—completely missing the target. We can treat issues and problems in the same way—we aim for the heart of the matter, but we land all over the place, far from the true issue. Sometimes we miss the target altogether.

I offer you a few examples from my coaching work of people missing the target:

What the caller said: "How can I get my kids to behave?"
The real problem: *My husband and I don't agree on how to discipline our children.*

What the caller said: "My boss is a jerk, and I'm miserable at work."
The real problem: *I struggle with some personality types and need help in getting along with people in the workplace.*

What the caller said: "I'm unhappy in my marriage and want out."
The real problem: *We argue about a lot of different things, and we need to seek marriage counseling. I know we really do love each other and both want to make this work.*

What the caller said: "My credit card interest went up, and I can't keep up with my bills."
The real problem: *I need to pay off my credit cards quickly and never use them for impulsive purchases again.*

What the caller said: "My wife makes lots of high-calorie meals and I'm putting on weight."
The real problem: *I like my wife's cooking, and I need to take responsibility for what I eat.*

Can you see how identifying the real problem can make all the difference in the outcome? As you begin considering the issue or challenge in your personal or family life that you want to address first, ask yourself each of these important questions:

- Is this really the problem?
- Is there more to this problem?
- What is really behind this problem?
- What have others said to me about this area of my life?
- What has God said about this area in his Word or in my prayer time with him?
- What is my role in the problem?
- Have I been blaming others for this problem?

Once you believe you have gotten to the root of the issue, ask God to give you wisdom and discernment to know if you've correctly identified the area you need to work on or if you need to look deeper.

b. *Understand the cost.* There is a cost to everything. There is a cost to action; there is a cost to inaction; there is a cost to solving a problem; there is a cost to not solving a problem. So whether you nail the issue and begin to make that first change or get sidetracked on a surface matter, there will be a cost. If you decide to courageously face the truth of an issue and your part in it, the solution will cost some time and effort—though with significant payback. If you get sidetracked, you'll continue getting the same results and consequences. Either choice is expensive. Are you willing to pay the price to improve your life?

Successful people prevail because they are willing to pay a lower price now instead of putting things off until later when the cost will be much higher. There is always a cost—spiritual, relational, emotional, physical, or financial—and sometimes all five.

If I choose to get a chocolate shake from the drive-through a couple of times each week, I not only pay the cost of the ice cream, I may also pay the cost of a few pounds gained each month. If I resist temptation and don't get the shake, I will pay the lower price of not enjoying the shake for five minutes or so, but the long-term result will be better.

c. *Do a reality check.* Now take a minute to turn your eyes away from the problem you've identified and take a look at yourself—not at your spouse or your child or your sister-in-law or your neighbor. Ask, "God, how have I failed in the past when I tried to address this? Where have I stumbled? What are my weaknesses? What patterns in my life have kept me from successfully changing before? Help me to truly understand the problem and understand myself so I can change the pattern I have followed in the past."

It is essential to identify and deal with unhealthy ruts or patterns in your life. In fact, the remaining chapters in this book will help you use the power of one thing to intentionally start making changes in some of the most troubling areas of life. You can do this, and in the chapters to follow I'll show you how.

Let's return to the man who called the program contemplating a move from Montana to Ohio. His misidentification of the true problem had already cost his family. His teenagers had experienced relational costs each time they were uprooted. The family had suffered financial and emotional costs because of the instability and disappointment of one job loss after another. Now he wondered if yet another move would improve things.

As I tried to guide his thinking to the deeper issues behind his job losses, he stubbornly clung to the need to move. "Once we're living near the in-laws and my wife can spend more time with them, the stress will let up and I'll be able to focus on getting a new job," he said.

Sadly, he wasn't yet willing to look beneath the current situation at the core problem behind his inability to hold on to a job. While many people lose employment through no fault of their own—whether because of layoffs, economic factors, or outsourcing, to name just a few—the pattern this man had experienced, especially having been fired from five jobs in a row, indicated a need for a closer look at his attitude and behavior to discover why he could not keep a job.

2. **Face your problem squarely and commit to making the necessary changes.** Want to know the secret to living an intentional life? It's as simple as the following formula:

Information + Insight + Action = Intentional Living

Information represents the facts you need to know about your situation—you need to know the total of all your debts, how high your blood pressure is, or what grades your struggling child is getting in school. Before you can make improvements, you need the facts, the information. *Insight* is being able to look at a problem in an analytical and thoughtful way, asking God to give you wisdom and discernment so you know what to do or what course to follow. *Action* means you start doing something about the information and insights you have gathered. Without action, nothing happens. These three components make up intentional living.

The verse I hold up as the banner for intentional living is Ephesians 5:10 (*The Message*): "Figure out what will please Christ, and then do it." Eugene Peterson's paraphrase gets it exactly right. Information plus insight plus action equals intentional living. That's what Paul commands us to do in this verse. Embrace his words for yourself and watch your life change.

So how might this play out in your own life? Let's say your doctor just told you that you need to lower your cholesterol and you know that exercise improves health (information). Next you realize that you have been allowing work and other commitments to crowd out any time for exercise in your schedule (insight). You then commit to walk for thirty minutes every day over your lunch hour, starting today, and you follow through on your commitment (action). Clearly, you are doing something good for yourself, for your health, and by extension, for your family, job, and finances (health care is very expensive).

Perhaps your goal is to pray more regularly. You know you must read God's Word and pray in order to know him better and do what he wants you to do (information). You've come to understand that, just as you would spend time with a friend or loved one you want to know and understand better, you need to spend time with God on a regular basis (insight). You then commit to pray more, scheduling time to do so starting this every morning (action).

Make your one thing small at first—small but consistent. If you want a stronger prayer life, you might commit to pray for five minutes after breakfast every day or in the car on your way to work. You might find it difficult at first to think of five minutes' worth of material to pray about. But do it anyway, no matter how you feel about your prayer experience. Don't be surprised when your five minutes of prayer grows to ten, twenty, or more minutes without your even realizing it.

Do the right one thing until it becomes a new habit. This usually requires about three or four weeks of consistent daily discipline. Your conversations with God will become more natural, and you might find yourself talking to him spontaneously throughout the day. Before you know it, your perspective about life will change. You will notice yourself becoming more thankful, more empathetic, and more able to see people as God must see them. Your desire for God's Word will grow.

If our caller had committed to applying this formula, he would have begun by evaluating the core problem. Let's say that the focus at all his exit interviews had been on his inability to get along with his coworkers (information). He would have recognized that his family's tension was caused largely by his dysfunction at work (insight). Clearly his unhealthy work patterns—not the decision of whether or not to uproot his family again—would need to be the focus of his efforts. He then could go to his peers and to God for help in understanding what changes he needed to make to be able to hold on to a job (action). He could commit to learning and incorporating these new skills as he sought a new position.

(See the form on page 171, which you can photocopy as often as you'd like, for a helpful way to organize these ideas.)

3. **Create a list of all of the "one things" necessary to get you to your goal.** Once you've correctly identified the problem and committed yourself to change, you have one other important step to take: namely, turn your problem into a goal to be reached. A problem without a goal is a problem that doesn't get fixed. Here are a few examples of how someone might turn a problem into a goal:

The problem: I'm too deep in debt.
The goal: To become debt free within three years

The problem: I'm overweight.
The goal: To lose twenty pounds by the end of the year

The problem: My wife and I don't get along.
The goal: To improve our marriage through counseling and agreeing to solve problems together

The problem: My teenager won't listen to me.
The goal: To develop a parenting plan of action and follow it daily

Once you have your goal statement, it's time to make a list of the "one things" necessary to get you to your goal. This list will become your action plan for intentional living. I encourage you to simply get out a piece of paper on which you write "My Goal" or "My Vision." It might be "I want to be a better parent," "I want to get out of debt," or "The one thing I want to focus on is my health." Underneath, make a list of the things you have to do to make that goal a reality.

The "one things" aren't listed so you can take care of all of them tomorrow. Rather, they are a plan for getting you to your goal. Start on the first thing on the list and keep working on it until it has become a habit or you feel confident that you have made a lasting change in that area.

Don't forget: *When starting out, tackle just one thing first, rather than trying to make several changes at once.* Go step-by-step through the items you've identified that will get you to your goal. Work on each one until it has become a habit or you have completed it.

For instance, if you have decided that your goal is to get out of debt within three years, here are some things you might include on your list:

I will record everything I spend for the next four weeks.

I will add up every expense and decide which ones are absolutely necessary and which ones could be dropped in the future.

I will create a simple spending plan based upon what I've learned. The spending plan will include giving 10 percent, saving 10 percent, and living on the balance.

I will find an accountability partner, someone with whom I can review my plan.

I will meet with my accountability partner once each month until my new habits become permanent.

Our caller might have listed the "one things" he needed to do to get a new job, such as:

I will make an appointment with my last employer to get honest feedback on areas in which I could improve—and I'll really listen to what he has to say.

I will read a self-improvement book on developing better interpersonal skills.

I will itemize other new skills I can learn to help me get a better job.

I will list where I can obtain those skills, such as a local community college or an online course.

I will update my résumé.

> I will study newspaper and online job postings and find those
> that match my skills and experience.
> I will submit my résumé.
> I will network with people in industries I am interested in and
> qualified for to get more information about opportunities.

Many people skip this simple step, jumping toward their goal without considering the steps required to make it a reality. Listing each of the steps required to accomplish a goal is well worth the time and effort.

4. **Begin doing the first thing on your list!** Once you've decided on your first "one small thing"—or even a series of small things— don't just sit there. Do that first thing, and don't be discouraged by the distance you need to go. If you have difficulty getting started, consider finding an accountability partner or scheduling time each week to evaluate the progress you're making.

   Once you've nailed that first thing, do the next thing on your list. You'll be working systematically, step-by-step, which will lead to success in that one big thing. In time, you may not always need to complete one thing before starting the next. Just commit to getting each "one thing" done—even if you have more than one thing in motion at a time.

5. **Review and revise your list as you go along.** As you start to work through your list of "one things," you may suddenly realize, *Wow! I left out some things,* or *This next thing is not something I should do.* Just stop what you are doing, then go back and rework your list. You can insert items or move things around. Just make sure that the next thing you do is the right thing, the thing that needs to happen now.

   For example: Let's say you are developing your budget. As you begin working through your steps, you realize the real problem is that you and your spouse are not on the same page financially. Maybe your spouse wants to save less or give more. I would encourage you to stop and make the next "one thing" you do resolving the conflict between you and your spouse. Working too far ahead will create confusion and discouragement.

But whatever you do, don't stop! There should always be another "one thing" in front of you to promote progress. Please don't allow inertia or critical people to keep you from moving forward. As Josh Billings said, "Observe the postage stamp! Its usefulness depends upon its ability to stick to one thing until it gets there."

Our caller needs to stick to his plan to get a new job, continuing to upgrade his interpersonal skills so he won't have to uproot his family again. This will reduce the likelihood that he will lose his sixth consecutive job.

Your "one things" will accumulate and grow into all sorts of benefits, some of which you might not even expect. But it's important to keep track of what you've done in a journal. Each time you notice a benefit, jot it down somewhere—in a notebook or on your computer—anywhere you can compile the list and find it easily. This record will encourage you in the low times that are a natural part of any plan or effort to change.

In part 2, I will introduce you to nine roadblocks to living an intentional life, and I will show how you can use the power of one thing to knock down each one.

The nine roadblocks to living an intentional life are:

1. Your thinking
2. Your attitude
3. Your emotions
4. Your words
5. The use of your time
6. Your friends
7. Your clutter
8. The questions you ask
9. The decisions you make

Get ready—you are about to experience the power of one thing done intentionally to change your life.

PART TWO

It's Time to Start— Change Your Life One Thing at a Time

5
THE POWER OF ONE THING TO CHANGE YOUR THINKING

You become what you think about, most of the time.
—BRIAN TRACY, BUSINESS CONSULTANT, WRITER, AND SPEAKER

Leslie, a graduate school student, had begun her advanced course work in the sciences with great enthusiasm. Several months into it, though, she was miserable. She dreaded going to class, particularly on test days. She spent hours in the lab, carefully setting up and monitoring every detail of each of her experiments. Often she woke up suddenly in the middle of the night, her mind racing and her heart pounding. What if she failed the next exam? How would she handle a setback in her research? How would she ever pay for the next semester? Her thinking was running wild and taking over her life.

Though her worry centered on school, Leslie brought this anxiety home with her. Her husband, Michael, generally felt the brunt of her irritation and short temper. He became frustrated at the way she constantly shrugged off his reassuring words and blew up whenever he offered a possible solution.

To their family and friends, it may have appeared that Leslie and Michael's marriage was shaky. Whenever they went out with family or friends, Leslie seemed preoccupied and Michael seemed angry. No doubt both partners needed to learn how to become more sensitive and understanding. However, after losing a third consecutive night's sleep over a botched lab experiment, Leslie had to face the fact that *she*—or more specifically, her thinking—was her biggest problem. Her tendency was to focus on all the bad things that could happen, which was taking a serious toll on her health and her marriage.

41

What about you? What have you been thinking about today? Studies show that people have anywhere from twenty thousand to sixty thousand thoughts a day—that's about one a second! The interesting thing: 95 percent of those thoughts are the same ones they had the day before. In the morning, you might think about what you're going to wear or how long the line at Starbucks will be. Those thoughts are pretty innocuous. But sometimes our thinking can become self-destructive, working against our well-being and dragging us down. It's not surprising that as Leslie began to worry about her odds of succeeding in graduate school, her thinking quickly spiraled downward.

Our ability to think and reason is one of the things that separates us from those in the animal kingdom. Being made in the image of God, humans have cognitive abilities possessed by no other species. As René Descartes said, "I think, therefore I am." Yet only we can determine whether our thinking will help or hinder us. In fact, we could modify Descartes' statement to say, "I am what I think," because from our thoughts come our words, behaviors, and actions—for good or ill. The power of one thing to change your life starts with getting control of your thinking—one day, one thought, one truth at a time.

Proverbs 23:7 (NKJV) says, "As [a man] thinks in his heart, so is he". Do you know what the context of that little proverb is? The previous verse says, "Do not eat the bread of a miser"—a cheapskate, a guy who doesn't want to share anything—"nor desire his delicacies; for as he thinks in his heart, so is he. 'Eat and drink!' he says to you, but his heart is not with you." In other words, the most important thing isn't what we say to others or how we act. We might invite someone to share a meal with us, but if we do it grudgingly, we really aren't being generous after all. Our thoughts determine who we really are.

I am what I think.

God takes our thoughts seriously, as the apostle James points out: "He who doubts is like a wave of the sea driven and tossed by the wind. For let not that man suppose that he will receive anything from the Lord; he is a double-minded man, unstable in all his ways" (James 1:6-8, NKJV).

Being double-minded means saying one thing while actually thinking another. It's a form of dishonesty. One of the greatest gifts we can give to ourselves, as we live an intentional life, is to be sure our thinking matches what we believe and then to start behaving in line with those truths.

Obviously, thinking is internal—it's beyond others' comprehension. Only you know what you are really thinking, and you become what you think about most of the time. You might have heard someone say, "You are what you eat" when talking about healthy eating, but I think a truer statement is, "You are what you think."

When I think about the difference between people who are successful—those who are balanced and satisfied in the key areas of life—and those who aren't, it often comes down to what they choose to think, and then in turn, what they choose to do. Successful people think harder, longer, and more clearly about fewer things—and then they act accordingly.

ONE THING

During your quiet time, meditate on one aspect of God's character, such as his power, majesty, or mercy.

Unsuccessful people think about a lot of different things and do little about them. When faced with a problem or setback, these people ask why—as in "Why do these things happen to me?" "Why did she talk to me like that again?" "Why can't my kids behave like other kids do?" Notice they're focusing on the problems (also known as worrying). Successful people, on the other hand, ask, "What can I do about it?" They focus on solutions.

What does this look like? Let's say you are meeting a good friend for lunch. Just before you pull in to the parking lot, your boss calls to say that a prospective client has asked for an extensive overhaul by next week on a proposal you drafted. After joining your friend at a table, you might let him or her chatter on as you internally fume. You nod at all the appropriate times, but you're actually remembering how you spent an entire weekend trying to get that report just right. You're sure your spouse is going to scream if you do that again. You mentally list all the items on your to-do list and wonder how you'll ever find time to revise the report. You wonder whether your boss will pass you over the next time a proposal needs to be written.

Focusing on the problem is usually our first inclination. But there is another way. Shifting from focusing on the problem to focusing on finding a solution is the only way to ultimately fix a problem or reach a goal. So let's consider another way to handle that lunch hour with your friend. You might still feel irritated as you enter the restaurant, but you remind yourself that at least the client has provided extensive feedback you can use to revise the report. You pick one item on your to-do list that can be postponed until the following week. You tell yourself you're going to enjoy lunch with your friend.

Would you rather spend time with people who focus on their problems or those who move ahead to get things done? Finding problems is easy—they are everywhere. But it's easy to slip into negativity if you're more apt to spot and point out a problem than to look for solutions to problems or good things to be thankful for. And it's easier to keep worrying about a problem rather than applying a bit of wisdom or a God-given principle to it. But doing so always leads you to a dead end.

On my national radio program, *Intentional Living*, I spend a lot of time talking with callers about their problems and how they can begin to solve them. Sometimes we call them back a few months later to see how they're doing. To my dismay, I've discovered that very few ever really apply what we've talked about. I've discovered that's because it's easier to dwell on problems than it is to focus on the solutions. It's one reason I'm so passionate about intentional living.

By focusing on *why* and endlessly pondering the answer to this unanswerable question, we fail to do anything to make the situation better. In light of all the blessings God gives us—including the ability to live, breathe, and wake up each morning, not to mention the ability and opportunity that most of us have to get a job and earn a living—the question is really, why has God chosen to be so generous and gracious and lavish in the way he deals with us? Job, who knew a lot more about suffering than most of us do, asked, "Shall we indeed accept good from God and not accept adversity?" Job 2:10 (NASB).

Instead of continually asking why you always seem to struggle in your life, in your marriage, with your kids, or in your personal walk with Christ, make a shift in your thinking. In a spirit of thanksgiving, start focusing on what you can do to improve things, what actions you can take, and the blessings you already have—tell yourself the truth.

Thinking is a spiritual discipline. Remember the apostle Paul's admonition in 2 Corinthians 10:5 that we take captive every thought to make it obedient to Christ? That's a command. It's a discipline for us to take control of our minds. Test your thoughts. Have you ever done that? In Philippians 4:6, Paul tells us, "Do not be anxious about anything." Then he adds: "You'll do best by filling your minds and meditating on things true, noble, reputable, authentic, compelling, gracious—the best, not the worst; the beautiful, not the ugly; things to praise, not things to curse" (verse 8, *The Message*).

Every thought that goes through your mind needs a little test:

- Is this truth?
- Is this honoring God?
- Is this taking me in the right direction?
- Is this going to accomplish the things that are most important in my life?

Here's one thing you can do: when you sit down and focus your thoughts in a positive way—solving problems, remembering God's goodness, focusing on the good things that can happen, understanding how the Bible applies to your life—then you "can do all things through Christ who strengthens [you]" (Philippians 4:13, NKJV).

ONE THING

Test each negative thought you catch yourself dwelling on. Don't accept it before asking yourself, *Is this truth? Will it take me in the right direction?*

Start telling yourself the truth. Intentional living demands it. Surely you wouldn't purposely lie to yourself, right? But we do it all the time— when we tell ourselves it was someone else's fault or we wouldn't have had that extra helping except for the tough day at work or we won't drink or smoke anymore after just one more. It's unproductive to focus on half-truths, negative self-talk, or gossip. Philippians 4:8 tells us to think about what is true: You are not a victim of your circumstances. You are not a victim of your past. You are not a victim of what's going on today.

Commit to the one thing of telling yourself the truth, even if it's painful or hard to do. God will help you to do that. Jesus said, "I am the way, the truth, and the life" (John 14:6, NLT). Focusing on the truth is the way to get your mind under control.

So how do you get your thinking straight? The Bible tells you to "pray without ceasing" (1 Thessalonians 5:17, NKJV), meaning you are to continually focus on Christ and his Word. If you want a good marriage, you need to focus on your marriage. If you want success on the job, you need to focus on success. In Psalm 86:11 David prays, "Teach me your way, O LORD, and I will walk in your truth." Focusing on God's thoughts, as expressed in the Bible, is the way to get your thinking straight.

Of course, lifelong thought patterns don't just magically go away when we start praying and reading the Bible. But over time and as we diligently apply what we read and learn in obedience, destructive patterns can be replaced with healthy ones that are in keeping with God's plan for our thought lives. We begin to focus on solutions rather than problems.

As I mentioned earlier, successful people focus on fewer things than unsuccessful people do, but they focus on the important things every day, day in and day out. In a poll we conducted on our *Intentional Living* radio program, nearly four hundred people responded to the question, "How much time in the average day do you pull away from your activity—your routine, your kids, your work, your spouse, all the things that you are doing—and think deeply about the most important issues of your life?" Forty-one percent said they spend less than ten minutes a day thinking about the most important issues of their lives. That's less than one percent of their time—less than one minute out of one hundred that they focus on the things that are most important in their lives. Seventy-six percent said they spend less than thirty minutes a day, or less than 3 percent of their time, focusing on the most important things in their lives.

Is it any surprise that we have mediocre lives, that we feel trapped and without the knowledge to raise our kids, that our most important relationships are filled with problems? We are not stopping to think about our priorities and how we can act to improve our lives in those areas. Intentional thinking is the focus of Romans 12:1, in which Paul tells us that we are to give our bodies as living sacrifices; in other words, through an act of our will, we are to give ourselves to Christ. Verse 2 adds that we are to be transformed by the renewing of our minds. But many of us, although we are followers of Jesus Christ and love God with all our hearts, still think incorrectly, which leads to mediocrity—or worse—in our lives.

Before we go further, let me emphasize that I'm not implying that we need to think our way into heaven or greater spirituality. You and I are saved for eternity because of what Jesus Christ did for us on the cross— yet we can still live mediocre lives because of lousy thinking. A lot of people with messed-up thinking will get into heaven, yet they may never experience success at those things that matter most to them in this life.

Leslie made a life-changing decision the day she recognized how toxic her thinking had become. She determined to change her thinking and stop dwelling on her negative thoughts. As soon as she recognized a harmful thought, she chose to bring to mind a hope-giving promise from Scripture, such as Zechariah 4:6: "'Not by might nor by power, but by my Spirit,' says the LORD Almighty."

ONE THING

List the most important issues and areas of your life on a personalized "thinking list."

In fact, I learned about her decision when she called in after I'd asked listeners to comment on the one thing that had put them on the road to intentional living.

As Leslie discovered, intentional living, which is all about knowing your purpose and living your purpose one thing at a time every day, requires you to be action oriented, even in your thinking. If your thoughts are bringing you down, I'd like to suggest some ways to help you identify the first "one thing" you need to do.

1. **Create your own thinking list.** The first step is determining your priorities. What should you spend time thinking about? Get a piece

of paper or your journal and list topics that represent the deepest concerns in your life. What matters most to you? Are there things you would think about if you had time? Are there issues you simply avoid thinking about because they are too painful or you feel hopeless about them? All of those things belong on your list. If you were to think deeply about that list, pray about those things, and then take action on those things, the result would be very positive.

ONE THING

Keep a gratitude journal in which you list at least one blessing each day.

Your personal thinking list contains the important issues and areas of your life. Only you can determine what those are. But once you have your list and have committed to telling yourself the truth, here are some additional self-assessment questions.

a. How real is God in my daily life, and how is that affecting me today?

b. How do my childhood memories affect my life today, and what will I do to grow beyond them?

c. What concerns me most about the direction of my life, and what needs to change?

d. What are my intentions for the future? Where would I like to be in five years? ten years?

e. Is my prayer life what it needs to be? If not, what am I going to do about it?

f. What legacy will I leave? Am I headed in that direction now?

2. **Capture your thoughts for personal growth and prayer.**
As you begin taking time to think through the truly important issues of your life, write down your thoughts to help you order and organize them. If you ever feel like your mind is racing or

you think you'll lose a good thought you just had, writing it down will help.

One advantage of journaling is that it takes all the jumbled thoughts in your mind and forces them out of the pen—one word at a time. For one split second as you write a word on your piece of paper, that word is your only thought. During the writing process, all other thoughts will likely get squeezed out of your mind, providing focus.

Writing will also help you identify thought patterns over time as you reread what you've written. You will identify areas of importance that come up again and again in your journal. After a while you might say, "Hey, I see that same word, that same feeling, that same thought, that same issue, or that same problem; it keeps coming up. It must be important."

The following outline offers a simple way you can begin capturing these thoughts:

WHAT MATTERS MOST TO ME:

Day 1 reflections on this topic:

_____

_____

_____

Day 2 reflections on this topic:

_____

_____

_____

THINGS I NEED TO THINK ABOUT WHEN I HAVE TIME:

Day 3 reflections on this topic:

_____

_____

_____

Day 4 reflections on this topic:

_____

_____

_____

ISSUES I AVOID THINKING ABOUT:

Day 5 reflections on this topic:

_____

_____

Day 6 reflections on this topic:

_____

_____

_____

3. **Schedule time to think every day.** What you thought about yesterday is shaping your life today. That means you can affect your tomorrow by what you choose to think about today. The list you create is a great starting point. But if you don't sit down with that list and schedule time to think through the critical parts of your life, it won't happen.

   If reasons why you can't do this are running through your mind (*I need to work. I've got kids. I've got a spouse. I've got a life. I've got a million things to do.*), set those thoughts aside for a minute. We all have the same twenty-four hours in every day, and those hours fill up almost by themselves unless we prioritize what we will spend our time on. Maybe the next "one thing" you need to do is spend time today thinking deeply about your life. If you don't schedule the time, it won't happen.

   Put your thinking time on your calendar or in your BlackBerry with a reminder alarm so you will be reminded when it's time to get out the list.

4. **Take control of your thinking!** Neglecting to schedule time is one reason many people don't think productively. Another reason may surprise you: it takes work to get focused. An undisciplined mind is a dangerous place. Often it's controlled by our runaway emotions. When we are struggling with anger or resentment or pride, it's likely that we are letting our thoughts and emotions control us.

Many people call my program and ask, "How can I deal with anger in my life?" I tell them that it starts in their minds. People don't typically explode in anger without having a quick thought just before that serves as a warning. If they tell themselves the truth—*I'm not a victim; I can do all things through Christ*—and commit to get help to learn to pause before responding, they can rein in their anger.

Have you ever asked your kids, "What were you thinking?" when they decked a classmate or got detention for talking back to a teacher? Well, the fact is they weren't thinking at all. That's why I always tell people, "It's not your first thought you should go with; it's your second thought." Usually the second thought will be a little more godly and a little more focused on your true values.

ONE THING

Adopt the habit of praying without ceasing by keeping Christ and his Word at the forefront of your mind.

If you don't discipline your mind, that first thought will tend to go right to the things that are not healthy for you—the old patterns of behavior, the old patterns of thinking, and so on. Mediocre lives begin with mediocre thinking.

So how do you begin to use your thinking time productively? First, learn to align your thoughts with what God has for you. Your thoughts need to be his thoughts. Is this even possible? It is for believers who, as Paul points out, "have the mind of Christ" (1 Corinthians 2:16). And once we align our thoughts with Jesus' thoughts, we no longer allow all the random thoughts and worries that enter our minds to control us.

Second, begin to meditate on your thoughts. For instance, have you ever taken a thought and just sat down to ponder it?

The intentionality of God
That God intentionally loves us
That God intentionally wants to help us
That God will help us live intentionally every day

Every great invention, every great accomplishment began with a thought. Bill Gates has said that early on in his life he could picture a computer on every person's desk in the world. He held on to that thought. Every building you have seen, every ministry, every church—everything in this world started with a thought from someone. It didn't just happen.

If your negative or unproductive thinking is hampering you, use the ideas in this chapter to select the one small thing you can begin doing right away so that your thoughts work for you and not against you. You might also choose from one of the possible action steps below. Once you've mastered one, go on to another.

ONE SMALL THING TO BEGIN CHANGING YOUR LIFE

- Schedule a time and a place to think. If you don't schedule it, it won't happen. Find a time when you will focus on nothing but thinking, and get it on your calendar. Then consider the best place for you to think—whether in a certain room or while you exercise or as you drive to work.

- Get out your thinking list and topics and go through them one by one in the amount of time you have. Stop on the one you're most concerned about today and meditate on it, pray about it, and find a verse from the Bible that applies to it.

- Keep writing in your journal or on your thinking list. Write down your thoughts and perceptions about what God is teaching you and telling you. Ask yourself, *What does this mean?* and *What should I do about this thought? Do I have a responsibility to do something? Is there something about this thought I need to share with other people?*

■ Act on at least one of your good thoughts. Pick one of the thoughts you have as you reflect on your list, and act on it. It could be small or life changing, and it could revolutionize your life.

■ Whenever you notice yourself starting to worry, stop and ask yourself, *Am I dwelling on the problem, or am I working on a solution?* Chances are, you're focused on the negative. Deliberately choose to think about possible solutions or, if the solution is out of your control, pray to God about it.

6
THE POWER OF ONE THING TO CHANGE YOUR ATTITUDE

The last of the human freedoms—to choose one's attitude in any given set of circumstances, to choose one's own way.
—VIKTOR FRANKL, *MAN'S SEARCH FOR MEANING*

Janet dreads extended family gatherings because, as she put it, "My mom and my sister ruin the whole day by being so negative about almost everything. The two of them are alike, and I hate going to spend time with them sometimes. It drags me down, and I feel drained by the time I leave. They have been like this for as long as I can remember. When I was a child, most of our dinner conversations ended up with my mom criticizing somebody or other—a neighbor, family member, or pastor. And my sister has turned out to be negative too. My mom has mellowed some, but my sister is worse than ever. No matter what I bring up, she can find something to criticize—my kids are too loud, our mom and dad don't do enough to help her, her husband is lazy, or the church is boring. Whatever we talk about, she always finds something wrong with it.

"After about an hour together, I'm eager to get out of there. If we're having dinner together, I can't wait until we finish eating so I can get the kids and leave. It takes me a day after being with her to calm down. I don't want my kids being exposed to all this negative stuff every time we are together, but no matter how much I try to change the subject to something more positive, my sister drags up something negative. I keep thinking it will get better, but it never does."

Your attitude has a huge impact on your life. I've noticed that unsuccessful people always seem to find something wrong, even in good

55

times, while successful people strive for an attitude of gratitude, even in bad times.

Your outlook on life begins with your thinking—what you allow your mind to dwell on—and it shows up in your attitude—the way you anticipate what's coming next and the lens through which you experience life. Your attitude is how you choose to see life. Your attitude affects your relationships, your family, your job, your friends, and your view of yourself. It affects the way your manager views you and the way your spouse and children relate to you, particularly how open and honest they will be with you.

Perhaps as you read Janet's story, a negative person came to your mind—someone you dread seeing as you wonder, *What will she be complaining about today?* Or *What did I do wrong this time?* Maybe it's the sour look on her face; her loud, stomping steps as she walks toward you; or just memories of past run-ins with her that make you leery.

Contrast the sour person with the one who always seems to bring light and hope to a situation—the person who looks for something good in any circumstance or something to thank God for, including what he has done in the past in a similar troubling situation. When that person enters a room, you breathe a sigh of relief, anticipating help and hope just from his or her presence.

I know I want to be the person others are glad to see coming, not the one who is dreaded. How about you?

Your attitude will determine how successful you will be at accomplishing the most important "one things" in your life.

We will talk about two issues when it comes to attitude: improving your own attitudes and dealing with other people who have negative or destructive attitudes.

HALF EMPTY OR HALF FULL

God has given us the ability to control what we allow our minds to dwell on, which we talked about in the last chapter. I can't prevent a negative thought from ever entering my mind, but I can reject it when it does come. I can refuse to focus on it or to go over it again and again. What we think about determines what kind of attitude we will have.

For example, if I'm constantly thinking about how unfair life is because I don't have many material things or good health or satisfying relationships—you name it—it's unlikely that I am going to have a thankful attitude. Instead, I'm probably going to have a complaining attitude that always notices what's wrong, what I don't have, and what wrongs have been done to me. If, on the other hand, I focus my thoughts on all the good things God has done for me and on the many needs of others, I will be thankful. By controlling or at least managing my thoughts so that they stay on productive things, I influence my attitude.

Just as God has given us a choice about what we will keep our thoughts on, he has given us a choice as to what our attitude will be. One of the best things we can do for ourselves is to have an attitude adjustment. We are not born with a negative attitude, although we might learn one at an early age if one of our parents is critical, complaining, or bitter. But even if we learn negative thinking, we can actually choose and train ourselves not to indulge in it. That's great news, isn't it? You don't have to be grumpy and angry all the time, criticizing those around you and making them and yourself miserable.

But saying we are going to change our attitudes and then actually doing so are two different things. In the parable of the two sons in Matthew 21, one son said he would not go into the vineyard and work as his father had asked, but he changed his mind and later went out to the field. The other son said he would go, but he didn't. Jesus said what matters most is changing one's mind and doing the right thing.

> "What do you think about this? A man with two sons told the older boy, 'Son, go out and work in the vineyard today.' The son answered, 'No, I won't go,' but later he changed his mind and

ONE THING

Listen in on your internal dialogue—and change the script when necessary. Choose a phrase like *I should have* . . . or *I'm so dumb* or *You never* . . . and resolve to eliminate it from your vocabulary.

went anyway. Then the father told the other son, 'You go,' and he said, 'Yes, sir, I will.' But he didn't go.

"Which of the two obeyed his father?"

They replied, "The first." (vv. 28–31, NLT)

Saying we'll do something without following through, as the second son did, is pretty meaningless. But if we start off wrong, as the older son did, and then change our minds, we can get it right. Are you willing to change your mind and your attitude?

First, think about your attitude toward yourself.

- Do you accept yourself as made by God for a good purpose and possessing great potential, or do you view yourself as a loser with little or no worth?
- What is your attitude toward your future?
- Do you believe you can work toward your goals and achieve them, or are you sure that nothing good is ever going to happen to you and that with all your limitations you can never succeed? Even your work ethic is an attitude.
- Do you look to see what you can do to make a situation better or to get the job done? Or do you try to do as little as possible, hoping someone else will carry the task to fruition? Attitude shows up in our prejudices.
- Do you have a preconceived notion of what you expect from a particular racial or ethnic group, or even from a male versus a female?

Our attitude represents our outlook on life and on other people; it's the lens through which we see the world. And while we might fool ourselves into thinking that no one else will know what our attitude is toward an individual, a group, or a particular topic—it is very apparent to others through our facial expressions and our words.

We've all known individuals who consistently see the glass as half empty, who anticipate rain when the sun is shining, who can find gloom in even the best news. The lens of these people is a dark one—it clouds everything they see and casts a shadow on it.

Other people see the glass as half full, find the silver lining in every dark cloud, and find something to be thankful about even in the most trying circumstances. Their lens is a bright one that seems to add sunshine to everything they see.

Of course, we're not completely consistent—even grouchy people have something favorable to say once in a while, and even the most upbeat person gets discouraged occasionally. Usually, though, individuals are mostly one way or the other—their lenses either darken or brighten most of their view of the world.

ONE THING

Take a "media fast"— deliberately turn off the flow of bad news and use that time to consider God's wonderful promises or the good things in nature.

Which lens do you see out of most of the time? Do you know? If you're not sure, ask yourself the following questions:

- Am I better at finding what is right or what is wrong in most circumstances?
- Do I look forward to the future?
- Am I happy about the success of others?
- Am I better at anticipating problems or successes?
- Do I notice something good about nearly every day?
- Am I more likely to point out a positive trait or a mistake or a flaw in the people around me?

Be honest. It's not always bad to see through that dark lens, which can keep us from getting carried away with optimistic and unrealistic plans. And it's not always a good thing to see through the sunny lens because we might overlook pitfalls or danger as we focus on the bright side. We need balance, and I'm not suggesting that we become unrealistic—just people with great attitudes.

It's easy to allow a healthy shaded lens to slip into a perpetually negative viewpoint where nothing is ever good enough and cynicism always seems to show up in our conversations, thoughts, and beliefs. We might even hurt our loved ones and others around us with our sharp, faultfinding tongue.

Years ago I lived in Michigan with its long, hard winters. Whenever my car got stuck in a deep snowbank, I would rock my car back and forth to try to get some traction and free myself. Often I couldn't get out alone, but if someone came along and gave me a push, I was able to move the car forward again.

That's why, besides conducting a self-assessment, you'd do yourself a favor to ask someone close to you or an unbiased counselor to help you identify an attitude problem. And don't forget to go to the greatest Coach ever, through fasting and prayer, and ask him for his direction and insight about your attitude.

Many of us are blind to our attitudes, particularly if we have lived our entire lives seeing through a negative lens so that it feels natural and right. We know a problem exists in our lives, but we are pretty sure it's caused by others. We may even believe we're just good at discerning others' problems and consider a critical attitude a kind of spiritual gift.

AN ATTITUDE OF HEALTHY DISCONTENT

If you identify negative attitudes that are stifling your growth, I suggest adopting an attitude of "healthy discontent," which acknowledges there is a more productive way of relating that you can master. Rather than being complacent and telling yourself, *That's just the way I am; things have always been this way; I can't do anything about the way I see things*, refuse to settle for the status quo, and be optimistic about your ability to make things better. That's an attitude of healthy discontent.

The one thing you need to do in order to develop such an attitude is to allow yourself to feel the emotions that go along with the results of a poor attitude. If you don't easily recognize or experience your emotions, this can be very difficult. Get off by yourself to think about and experience your feelings, whatever they are. Ask God to help you understand yourself and your situation clearly so you can use your healthy discontentment with your life to propel you forward toward a better life.

Realize that a lousy attitude isn't predetermined by your genes; it's a personal decision each of us must make. Just because your parents or siblings have bad attitudes doesn't mean you have to. Every time you give in to a bad attitude, your negativity will increase, but thankfully, every time you do something to cultivate a positive attitude, that outlook will have greater control over your life. If you win enough attitude battles, you will win the attitude war.

KEEPING YOUR ATTITUDE UP WHEN SOMEONE ELSE'S THREATENS TO BRING IT DOWN

What do you do if, like Janet, you're around someone with a negative attitude? First, recognize that unless a person wants to change and asks for your help, you can't do a thing to improve someone else's attitude. A good attitude is an inside job that only the one with the attitude can fix. Janet cannot change her mom and sister, and the more she tries, the more disappointed and upset she will become.

I often share this formula with callers to our radio show:

Expectations – Reality = Disappointment

If we expect something that isn't realistic, we will be disappointed. It's a simple but profound concept. Since Janet cannot change the reality of her sister's attitude, she must accept her for the way she is. That won't mean that Janet will enjoy listening to her sister's negative comments, but it will help her realize that this is the way her sister is and that she can't change her. Janet can continue to love her, but she might have to draw boundaries that will protect her children from the constant barrage of negativity. She can also set an example by being thankful, optimistic, and positive—whether or not her sister ever agrees with her. And she can pray that her sister will develop an attitude of thankfulness for all God does for her every day.

ONE THING

Prepare and rehearse your response to negative talk from others—for instance, as soon as your chatty coworker starts gossiping about your boss, tell her that you need to get back to work.

Along with praying, before getting together with her sister, Janet can prepare and rehearse what she will do when the negative talk starts up. She can decide whether to confront her sister, try to change the subject, remove her children from the room, or set a good example by being positive. She might ask for support and guidance from other family members who could help her address the problem.

Would you say you're more like Janet or her sister? If a negative attitude is wearing you out, consider doing one thing today to begin turning your outlook around.

ONE SMALL THING TO BEGIN CHANGING YOUR LIFE

- Identify your triggers. If you tend to fall into negativity, consider what triggers this negative attitude in you.

- Decide precisely what you will do when you're tempted to say something negative. You may choose to change your physical position, get up and go for a walk, hug your kids or spouse, reach out and help somebody with an immediate need, or pray. Be creative.

- The next time your trigger occurs, do something different. Switching how you respond to a negativity trigger can help break the pattern.

- Whenever possible, hang around people with great attitudes. Learn from them, ask them what they do to keep a good attitude in difficult situations, and imitate what they do.

7
THE POWER OF ONE THING TO CHANGE YOUR EMOTIONS

The ruling passion, be it what it will,
The ruling passion conquers reason still.
— ALEXANDER POPE, EIGHTEENTH-CENTURY POET

Sarah, a district sales manager, believed that the best way to motivate her employees was through fear. She never hesitated to point out an error, usually in front of other people, and if someone disagreed with her, she often became angry. It wasn't unusual for an employee to leave Sarah's office in tears. But Sarah's team produced the top sales results three years in a row, and Sarah thought she must be doing something right by running such a tight ship.

At Sarah's annual performance review, her manager commented on her team's great sales results, saying, "Sarah, your employees are outselling the rest of the organization, but I've heard more than once that your people feel intimidated by your demands and anger."

"When they stop beating everyone else in sales, I'll start holding their hands more," Sarah said.

Her manager said, "I value your sales performance, but more than that, I value people, and your behavior isn't the way to treat employees. You're getting great results, but at what cost?"

Sarah could feel her face turning red as her heart rate sped up. "Are you telling me I'm not doing my job?"

"I'm telling you that you need to get your emotions in check if you're going to continue leading this team."

Sarah stormed out of her manager's office, slamming the door behind her.

Like Sarah, many of us need to manage our emotions. Our success in life may depend on it. Just consider these statistics on anger and related emotions from the British Association of Anger Management Web site:[4]

- 45 percent of British workers regularly lose their tempers on the job.
- 27 percent of nurses have been attacked at work.
- One in twenty people have had a fight with a person living next door.
- 80 percent of drivers say they have been involved in road rage.
- 50 percent of people have reacted to a computer problem by hitting the computer, throwing something across the room, screaming, or abusing a colleague.
- More than one-third of those in the United Kingdom lose sleep from anxiety. (I would think that's pretty typical on our side of the pond as well.)
- Depression and anxiety have overtaken physical ailments as the chief cause of long-term illness.

Runaway emotions can do more damage than just about anything else when it comes to relationships, families, finances, careers, and health. Runaway emotions have destroyed marriages and relationships, estranged families, ruined people's health, forced people into bankruptcy, and caused people to lose jobs. If you let them, runaway emotions will hijack your life.

ONE THING

Schedule time to exercise several times a week. Your aim isn't to become a world-class athlete but to release your emotions through physical activity.

In and of themselves, emotions are not bad or harmful. Emotions are given to us by God, so they are good. We experience joy over good things, sadness over loss, and anger at injustice. God gave us emotions to help us express ourselves, relate more deeply to others, and deal with various situations. Emotions can prompt us to act for good. When we have sympathy or pity for a suffering person, we can move to alleviate some of his or her pain.

Let's look at the word *emotion*. The prefix *e* in a word means "coming out of or from" (emigrating is leaving a country for another); the word *motion* means movement. In other words, emotions are a result of something happening to you that causes movement. They are a reaction to something. Emotions may seem to come from nowhere, but they always result from either an event or a thought, and they're always intended to take you somewhere. They have a point of origin, and they have a predetermined destination. Understanding the origin of your emotions and what they are trying to get you to do is one thing worth pursuing.

Unlike thoughts, which are cognitive activities that allow us to respond to life, emotions cause an automatic physical reaction, a bodily response. Consider how easy it is for you to discern what emotion I might be feeling if I told you I was having the following bodily reactions:

- I feel like I have butterflies in my stomach! (nervousness, excitement)
- I feel like I have a heavy weight on my shoulders. (stress, sadness)
- My heart is racing! (anxiety, anticipation)
- It feels like my blood is running cold. (terror, anger)

Emotions are a gift from God, and everyone experiences them. But as good as they are, like other aspects of our fallen nature, our feelings can easily get us off track. Successful people have learned to identify and control their internal state, and they know how to control their outward reactions. Often those who don't succeed either allow their emotions to dictate their reactions or attempt to repress their feelings completely. Good, healthy emotions that we let run out of control, or at the other extreme, try to repress completely, can lead to runaway emotions—emotions that are allowed to rule our lives.

You may be thinking, *I can't control what I feel. My feelings are just there.* It's true that you will naturally experience certain feelings or emotions in various situations. But how you handle them, and whether or not you keep them within healthy boundaries, is up to you.

Just as you can't keep a negative thought from popping into your mind but can choose whether to dwell on it or replace it with something more constructive, so you can decide whether to wallow in a legitimate but negative emotional response to a painful situation. We may feel sadness at the death of a loved one, and that is normal and good, a way of processing our grief. But if, after an extended period of time, our sadness has immobilized us so that we cannot function or relate to others or go to work, our sorrow has become a runaway emotion. It has stopped serving the healthy function God intended and has paralyzed us.

THE ORIGIN OF EMOTIONS

Several years ago I went to Jamaica with our ministry leaders to help those living in poverty. When most of us think of Jamaica, we think of Montego Bay or big cruise ships that stop in the ports or white sand beaches and clear blue water—the reasons vacationers go to the island. But those things are not the Jamaica I experienced.

I simply was not prepared for the emotional impact that experience would have on my life. The level of poverty surpassed anything I'd ever seen in the United States.

We landed in Kingston, Jamaica, and were taken to a secure hotel site in the city, although our ultimate destination and mission objective was the city garbage dump where hundreds of families lived. When we walked to the dump, I was absolutely stunned. Oozing trash came up to my ankles; the smell was awful. But hundreds, if not thousands, of Jamaican people call this squalid, reeking place home. In the midst of the garbage I saw an older woman living in a refrigerator box—everything she owned was in that box. When she turned her back, I quickly snapped a picture in order to remember that moment. That dump was where she lived. It was her home. Every time I see that picture it evokes an emotional response—one that reminds me of how many blessings we have here.

A typical home in the city dump in Jamaica is not like a home in the United States. A home there is literally the size of a toolshed, maybe ten by ten feet with a door and a hole with no glass for a window. It barely provides enough shelter to get families away from the filth and likely houses eight to ten people.

I could not even begin to comprehend how these people, including many precious little children, were living amid the filth and garbage. I felt great sympathy for them, but empathy—the ability to imagine what it must be like to walk in their shoes—eluded me. I simply couldn't relate because their life is so far outside my realm of experience. Still, I longed to help them, and as a ministry, we raised $100,000 to help build dozens of little homes for some of these people.

That trip changed my life and my perspective on the world. When I returned home, I was unable to explain to my wife, Donna, the emotional reaction I had experienced. I know you have had experiences like that also. In fact, if you are *not* moved by experiences like this, you have a problem. If a person can encounter extreme need or go through a tragedy numb and void of emotion, he or she probably needs to see a therapist or counselor for help.

While the source of some emotions is obvious, others are less so. Some are evoked by situations or external things that remind us of a past experience or feeling, such as something we tasted, heard, or smelled.

As I mentioned in chapter 3, I live in Arizona where there is little grass. Most of us have decorative rock in our yards. But every once in a while in the summer, I hear somebody in my neighborhood running a lawn mower to trim a little plot of grass.

That sound takes me back to Michigan, where I grew up. My childhood memories of mowing the lawn and smelling the grass clippings evoke an emotion; it's a warm feeling that takes me back to my youth. An emotion may also be triggered by some physical action. You might be tossing a ball and suddenly have a memory that takes you back to a time when you were a child doing that very same thing.

ONE THING

Restart an activity you loved doing as a kid. If your parents' budget forced them to drop the piano lessons you enjoyed, for instance, sign up to take them again. If you loved kickball, why not join one of the adult leagues springing up all over?

In 1978 I was in a serious car accident. It occurred at the corner of M-50 and Rives Junction Road, just north of Jackson, Michigan. As I pulled up to the corner of M-50, a major thoroughfare, I saw a vehicle waiting at a stop sign for traffic to clear from the busy intersection. Suddenly the driver pulled her van out right in front of an oncoming car. From my vantage point, I had seen the car coming quickly toward us, but the van driver couldn't see it. Everything seemed to move in slow motion as the approaching car came over the top of the hill at sixty miles an hour. The impact of the collision made the van roll over. Then both vehicles came right over the top of my car.

The accident was so violent that a table from the van was found more than three hundred feet away from the accident. All the vehicles were totaled. Although the accident occurred years ago, whenever I return to Rives Junction and drive up to that same intersection, my blood pressure goes up and my heart rate soars. If you ask me to name the most dangerous intersection in America, I will tell you M-50 and Rives Junction Road. That is because it evokes emotion for me.

Maybe you have experienced something like that too. That's because your emotions are tied to past experiences—the memories that impact your current beliefs about your life. An emotion is like a fire on the inside, and it burns until one of three things happens:

1. **The emotion can propel you into healthy responses to life.**
   Emotions always create reactions. Why are lie detector tests used? Because by measuring a person's heart rate, respiration, and pulse, experts can use physical reactions to detect anxiety and dishonesty.

   When you have an emotional response—anger, frustration, or hurt, for example—you may be propelled to do something good (which is a healthy response). Years ago I realized I needed to go to someone and apologize for something I had done. I hate having a breach between myself and another person, and an emotion told me something was not right between us. I chose to sit down with this person and say, "You know, in this situation I was wrong. Will you forgive me?" That was a healthy response to an emotion. When God gives you an emotion, use it wisely. Understand where it is coming from and what you need to do about it. People who respond correctly to their emotions will be emotionally healthy.

2. **The emotion can explode into an unhealthy reaction.** If you ignore your emotions, they grow from a small fire inside of you into an explosion. That's what happened to Sarah, the sales manager. Someone like her might know her reaction is wrong, but she doesn't think anyone really cares or that an apology will matter. She might even justify what she did or blame someone else for it. She often leaves a trail of broken and unhealthy relationships because she hasn't dealt with her emotions in a healthy way. Explosive people often keep you at a distance while being very controlling. Generally they will take no responsibility for problems and will not try to resolve a problem with another person.

3. **The emotion can smolder into a self-inflicted emotional wound.** Emotions may smolder under the surface. Christians, in particular, are prone to stuffing angry feelings inside instead of expressing them because they assume Scripture commands believers not to get angry. They may even quote passages like Psalm 4:4 (NLT), which says, "Don't sin by letting anger control you. Think about it overnight and remain silent."

Notice, though, that this verse isn't saying anger itself is wrong. It's only when we let it control us or allow anger to cause us to hurt another person with words or actions that we fall into sin. Instead, the psalmist advises us to process our angry feelings thoughtfully. If we try to stuff

> **ONE THING**
>
> Before responding to another person in an emotional situation, take at least ten seconds to consider his or her verbal and facial cues as a means of better understanding that person's perspective.

these feelings down inside, neither expressing them nor acting on them in a healthy way, they are likely to smolder inside and either harm our health or build up to an explosion toward others.

Not only can the resulting stress and depression take a toll on our bodies, but such a response also often leads to passive-aggressive behavior: saying nothing about an issue but taking it out on others in a quiet, subtle way. Smoldering people never let you know quite what they are thinking, but their emotions lead to controlling or manipulative actions.

When I see people in Florida and along the Gulf Coast whose lives have been devastated by recurring hurricanes, I find the differences in their emotional responses fascinating. Some have a determined reaction—they will stay and rebuild, despite the fact that their homes and all their belongings are gone. Others are fearful of trying to rebuild—what if the same thing happens again?—and they leave. Many are angry and blame the government for not responding quickly enough. Others simply trust God. All these people have gone through the same crisis, but their emotional reactions are very different. One healthy thing you can do is to correctly identify your pattern of response to different emotions—anger, fear, anxiety, loneliness, etc.

WHEN EMOTIONS BECOME A PROBLEM

When should you be concerned that you have an emotional issue that needs attention? When your emotions negatively interfere with any of the five important areas of your life. If you experience any of the responses to unhealthy emotions listed below, it's time for you to use the power of one thing to change them:

1. Faith
   a. distrust of God and his Word
   b. distance from God
   c. procrastination from reading the Word or being in prayer
   d. anger at God

2. Relationships
   a. discord with spouse, children, or other family members
   b. selfishness
   c. broken relationships or friendships

3. Health
   a. ulcers, high blood pressure
   b. fatigue, anxiety, depression
   c. overeating
   d. smoking, other addictions

4. Finances
   a. overspending
   b. hoarding
   c. instant gratification

5. Work/service
   a. lack of focus
   b. miscommunication
   c. lack of productivity
   d. workaholism

How to Change Your Emotions

Thinking is a precursor to everything that happens in our lives, so when we work on changing our emotional reactions, we need to go at the problem from both ends—our thoughts and our actions. Here are two of the most powerful "one things" you can start doing today to conquer an unhealthy emotion:

1. Start thinking like Christ, and you will change your emotions.
2. Start behaving like Christ, and you will change your emotions.

This is easier said than done, I know. In one of my favorite Scripture passages, Philippians 4:6, Paul says, "Be anxious for nothing." But he doesn't leave us hanging there, asking, "How?" He lays out exactly what we are to do—the actions to take—to become free from anxiety.

Be anxious for nothing, but in everything by prayer and supplication with thanksgiving let your requests be made known to God.

And the peace of God, which surpasses all comprehension, will guard your hearts and your minds in Christ Jesus. (Philippians 4:6-7, NASB)

Notice that Paul doesn't just order us to change our emotions. Instead, he says, "Do you want to get rid of that anxiety you are feeling? Then start right here. Take action, whether you feel like it or not." He tells us to pray and make our requests to God, always being thankful as we ask. And the promise is the peace of God! That's freedom from anxiety.

Paul continues with even more specificity as to the beginning of our process—thinking: "Finally, brothers, whatever is true, whatever is noble, whatever is right, whatever is pure, whatever is lovely, whatever is admirable—if anything is excellent or praiseworthy—think about such things" (Philippians 4:8).

So what else does it mean to think and act like Christ?

Thinking like Christ is one thing you can do

If you are not a Christian—if you do not know Christ—then I pray that you will come to know him. Read his Word, the Bible, and seek a relationship with him. He promises to reveal himself to anyone who earnestly seeks him (see Jeremiah 29:13).

For those of us who are followers of Christ, we must understand that positive thinking is not enough. Certainly it's a start, but we need to go beyond that and think like Christ. To be able to do that, we must go to the source, the Bible, where we find what Christ told us to think about. We read in Romans 12:2, "Do not conform any longer to the pattern of this world, but be transformed by the renewing of your mind. Then you will be able to test and approve what

ONE THING

In a Bible concordance or online searchable Bible, look up a word such as *shame* or *anxiety* that represents your greatest emotional struggle. Memorize one of the verses listed that contains a promise of God or an insight into dealing with that emotion. Bring it to mind whenever that emotion surfaces.

God's will is—his good, pleasing and perfect will." Get into the Word to understand what the Bible tells you about how to think. Here are some more verses where Jesus showed his thoughts through the words he said:

Have faith: "With man this is impossible, but with God all things are possible." (Matthew 19:26)

Follow Jesus: "Come, follow me . . . and I will make you fishers of men." (Mark 1:17)

Be a servant: "If anyone wants to be first, he must be the very last, and the servant of all." (Mark 9:35)

God will take care of you: "Do not worry about your life, what you will eat; or about your body, what you will wear. Life is more than food, and the body more than clothes. Consider the ravens: They do not sow or reap, they have no storeroom or barn; yet God feeds them. And how much more valuable you are than birds!" (Luke 12:22-24)

Have mercy and forgive: "If any one of you is without sin, let him be the first to throw a stone at her." (John 8:7)

Obey: "If you hold to my teaching, you are really my disciples." (John 8:31)

Through Jesus, you will have eternal life: "I am the resurrection and the life. He who believes in me will live, even though he dies; and whoever lives and believes in me will never die. Do you believe this?" (John 11:25-26)

We can see that Jesus' thoughts have a consistent theme. He knows who God is and that he keeps his promises. Jesus is a man of peace because he trusts implicitly in the Father. May we, too, have the mind of Christ, as we read in Philippians 2:5 (KJV): "Let this mind be in you, which was also in Christ Jesus."

Acting like Christ is another one thing you can do

You know the popular question, "What would Jesus do?" In the Bible you'll find out what Jesus did in fact do—in his relationships with people, in times of trouble and suffering, and in times of victory.

The Old Testament figure Joseph is often described as a forerunner of Christ. He is a great example of a man who thought like Christ and behaved like Christ. Joseph was emotionally and physically abused by his brothers, he was cast into prison, and his employer's wife wrongfully accused him. He had every reason to let emotional reactions derail his life. Rather than becoming consumed with bitterness, he chose to behave like God and think like God. He stayed the course and did the right thing, preparing Egypt for the coming famine. When his brothers had a food shortage, where did they go? They went to "homeland security" in Egypt to ask for help, never imagining that their long-abandoned brother would be there.

Think about the emotions you would feel in Joseph's position. When he saw his brothers for the first time in many years, Joseph could have thought, *Wow! I've got them where I want them now. Whatever goes around comes around.*

But listen to Joseph's words to his brothers:

> "Come close to me." When they had done so, he said, "I am your brother Joseph, the one you sold into Egypt! And now, do not be distressed and do not be angry with yourselves for selling me here, because it was to save lives that God sent me ahead of you. For two years now there has been famine in the land, and for the next five years there will not be plowing and reaping. But God sent me ahead of you to preserve for you a remnant on earth and to save your lives by a great deliverance. So then, it was not you who sent me here, but God. He made me father to Pharaoh, lord of his entire household and ruler of all Egypt." (Genesis 45:4-8)

Perhaps you've been thinking, *You don't know my situation, Randy. The things that have been done to me would make anyone bitter.* If so, ask yourself if the wrongs done to you equal being sold into slavery by your family or being thrown into jail because of a false accusation. Can the wrongs done to you compare with being crucified on a cross, as Jesus was, to pay for our sins?

Thinking and acting like Christ will free you to succeed, as Joseph discovered.

Dealing with our emotions is a daily battle. It's not something we master once and for all. Emotions constantly need our attention because they come unbidden—but it's up to us to decide how we will handle them.

You may have read the book *Emotional Intelligence* by Daniel Goleman.[5] He found that, more than IQ or intelligence, EQ or emotional intelligence is the primary predictor of a person's success in life. People who are emotionally intelligent are more successful than those who are only intellectually intelligent. We all know smart people who are dumb emotionally, don't we? Goleman lists five characteristics of emotionally intelligent people. As you read them, evaluate yourself on each one.

People who are emotionally intelligent:

1. **Are self-aware.** As I pointed out in chapter 3, understanding yourself is critical to making meaningful change in your life. Goleman said that at any given time, a self-aware person knows how he or she feels. If you were asked, in any situation, "How do you feel at this moment?" could you identify your feelings? Many people cannot. When I conduct marital counseling sessions, conversations sometimes become very heated. If one person becomes visibly angry or begins to shut down and withdraw, I often ask him or her, "How do you feel right now?" Often the person doesn't know or tells me something that really isn't true.

   Are you aware of your feelings right now? Are you aware of your feelings during a meeting at work or when you are talking to your spouse; when you are sitting in church on Sunday morning; when you are driving down the road and someone cuts you off? People who are self-aware are more emotionally intelligent—and more successful in life—than those who are not. Rate yourself on a scale of one to ten: How self-aware are you?

ONE THING

If you're not sure what you're feeling about a particular situation, use a journal to begin sifting through the thoughts and impressions that may help you uncover your emotions.

2. **Manage their moods.** Some people say, "I wear my emotions on my sleeve . . . that's just who I am." Nonsense! Emotionally intelligent people know how to manage their emotions—acting on those that are appropriate for each situation. They are not closed down, but they exercise appropriate emotional responses for the situation. They may feel angry, but they learn effective ways to express those feelings without attacking someone or blowing their stack.

   Rate yourself on a scale of one to ten: How well do you manage your emotions?

3. **Know how to self-motivate.** In his research, Daniel Goleman found that one of the key ingredients for motivating yourself is knowing how to delay gratification; in other words, having a goal that is bigger than your immediate pleasure. Dr. Walter Mischel of Stanford University did a study with four-year-olds in which he brought each child into a room and placed a marshmallow in front of him or her. He said, "Either you can have one marshmallow right now or you can have two if you wait until I come back."

   Then he left the room for fifteen minutes, which is an eternity for a four-year-old. His team videotaped the kids' responses and found that two-thirds of the kids waited and one-third took their marshmallows right away. When they watched the children who waited, they found that those children covered their eyes or turned their backs on the tempting treat. Many of us tend to trade away something better down the road for immediate gratification. We'd rather spend our money today than save it for later; we'd rather eat that chocolate cake than slim down gradually by reducing our consumption of such goodies.

   These children were tracked over the years, and thirteen years later, after they had graduated from high school, researchers discovered that those who had delayed their gratification as four-year-olds had significantly better SAT scores, were more socially adjusted, got better reports from their parents and teachers, and were more successful overall than those who had not delayed their gratification. Successful people know how to motivate themselves toward a larger goal and choose not to do everything they want to do right now.

Rate yourself on a scale of one to ten: How good are you at self-motivation?

4. **Are able to read people.** Empathy is the ability to get behind the eyes of another person and see and experience what he or she sees. It takes a willingness to get beyond self and care about what someone else is going through—not only hearing the words, but putting oneself into another's situation and imagining what it must be like. People who can read others have empathy because they are able to pick up on verbal, facial, and other cues, enabling them to see the situation from the other person's perspective. How empathetic are you?

Rate yourself on a scale from one to ten: How well do you read people?

5. **Can manage relationships.** Emotionally intelligent people have developed people skills, which are essential to emotional intelligence; they continually learn to get along with other people. How do you get along with others? Successful people are able to interact with many different kinds of people, putting them at ease and making them feel comfortable.

Rate yourself on a scale of one to ten: How well do you manage relationships?

Unlike the emotionally intelligent, unsuccessful people don't understand themselves very well; they live at the whim of their moods, and they may have difficulty motivating themselves and relating well to others. They also crave instant gratification.

Sarah's unwillingness to control her emotions around her subordinates explains why she, a skillful salesperson, failed when she was promoted to district sales manager. Not long after her annual review, one of Sarah's employees made a mistake in billing an account, and she let him have it during a team meeting. "How many times have I talked to you about those invoices? Can't you get it right? What's wrong with you?"

Her manager's words were but a distant whisper, and Sarah's runaway anger had its way.

The next day, the salesperson she had publicly berated—a top performer—turned in his resignation. Sarah was furious with the employee and left early. The next morning when she checked her phone messages, she heard her boss's request that she come to his office first thing. Her mistreatment of a valued team member, the result of runaway anger, was about to cost Sarah her job.

Your emotions are a huge part of your life. When you try to run from them, deny that you have them, blame others for them, or ignore them, you do so at a great risk to yourself and those you love. Your emotions will come at you daily because they are reactions to life that should prompt you to action—the right action.

If, after reading this chapter, you recognize that you have difficulty handling your emotions appropriately, beginning to do one small thing today for your emotional health could be the best move you make.

ONE SMALL THING TO BEGIN CHANGING YOUR LIFE

- Write down one emotion that you seem to experience more often than you'd like. Is it anger, sadness, despair?

- Think about the last time you experienced this emotion and how you handled it. Write down a brief description of the situation. Are you pleased with the way you handled it? What could you have done differently?

- Do you tend to go for instant gratification? For example, do you head to your favorite clothing store, ready to plunk down your credit card when your closet is already stuffed? Maybe you have a hard time passing up the doughnuts in your office even though you know you need to lose twenty pounds. Identify your vulnerable area, and come up with a strategy to help you resist it. You might decide to cut up that store credit card or find a route to your desk that doesn't take you past the break room and that box of doughnuts.

■ Rewrite the script for the last time you experienced an emotion you struggle with. What would it look like it if you had handled it as Jesus would have?

■ Break down the successful picture you just created into small steps and write them down. Here's an example:

1. My boss came to my desk and asked why I hadn't completed the XYZ project yet.

2. I felt anger rise within me, along with a stressed feeling.

3. I wanted to tell him that my workload is such that I can't possibly complete the XYZ project along with all my other work, blaming him for not managing my workload better—which, after all, is part of his job.

4. Instead, I asked if he and I could meet to talk about the project and what additional resources we might be able to gather to help get the work done.

5. He agreed to meet tomorrow, and I felt my blood pressure ease back down because I had responded positively, asking for the help I need, and avoided blaming or getting defensive.

■ Review the steps often and keep the paper with you in a pocket or wallet. Try to practice the successful scenario you envisioned the next time you feel stressed and angry.

8
THE POWER OF ONE THING TO CHANGE YOUR WORDS

Watch your thoughts, for they become words;
watch your words, for they become actions;
watch your actions, for they become habits;
watch your habits, for they become character;
watch your character, for it becomes your destiny!
—SOURCE UNKNOWN

Maria's husband, Thomas, blamed her for all his problems at work. If she were more encouraging, he told her, he would do better; if she were more supportive, he would have enough confidence to succeed; if she didn't take up so much of his time, he would be able to put in more hours at the office. As his difficulties at work mounted, his verbal attacks became more severe. Maria tried to support and encourage him, and she told him he could spend as much time at work as he needed to. She could take care of their two young children while he had to be gone.

During his second annual performance review at the company, Thomas was put on employment probation because of the inaccuracies in his work and his surliness with other employees. That night Thomas lit into Maria, telling her that he had to stick with his crummy position because she was too lazy and stupid to get a job. His rage at his employer, and perhaps at himself, boiled over, and she was the target.

Thomas apologized the next day, but he verbally demeaned her again a week later. The couple's young children became irritable and hyperactive, sensing the increasing trouble between their parents. Thomas's rage seemed to grow and grow, and Maria was just thankful it was directed at her and not at their children.

At the end of his employment probationary period, Thomas was let go from his job. He stopped for a couple of beers on the way home, and as he walked in the door, he was muttering about the unfairness of his company and Maria's lack of support.

When he came into the kitchen from the garage, the children were arguing with each other. Just then the little girl hit her brother, sending him into spasms of sobs. Maria started to separate the children and straighten out the problem, but Thomas intervened. "Maria, I slave all day and then I come home to find the kids out of control! Can't you even keep them quiet?"

Then, grabbing his daughter's arm, Thomas yelled, "Kaitlyn, if you hit your brother again, I'll give you a spanking you'll never forget!" Turning to his son, he said, "Tyler, stop that crying! Are you such a sissy you let your sister beat you up?"

Maria, so angry she was shaking, stepped in front of Thomas and said with all the control she could muster, "Thomas, you're scaring the children. I'm taking them upstairs."

Over the next few weeks, as Thomas unsuccessfully searched for a job, he became more and more verbally abusive. Finally, Maria had had enough. She and the kids moved in with her parents.

After she separated from Thomas, he became contrite. "You know I didn't mean what I said. I'm sorry. The whole job thing just got to me."

But it was too late for Maria. She said, "It all started when you blamed me for your troubles at work. The things you said to me and the kids slowly killed my love for you. I'm sorry, but it's over."

WORDS MATTER

You have more power over other people than you may ever have imagined. Unless you are a hermit living in complete isolation, every day you have the power either to spark enthusiasm or to kill it; to build confidence or to destroy it; to foster peace or to steal it. And the power you wield isn't something you must purchase or work for: it all comes down to the words you say. No wonder the psalmist teaches us to pray, "May the words of my mouth and the meditation of my heart be pleasing in your sight, O LORD, my Rock and my Redeemer" (Psalm 19:14). This verse confirms that our words matter. They are powerful. They change lives.

Successful people understand that words have the power to heal or to hurt, and they keep that in mind before they speak. Other people blurt out whatever they feel like saying with little regard for the consequences. When successful people realize they've used hurtful words, they don't make excuses. They think, *I blew it yesterday, but I'm going to speak differently today.* Other individuals repeat the same harmful messages over and over to those around them without ever acknowledging the damage they're doing.

But they're just words. You know, "Sticks and stones . . ." and all that. It's not like I've ever actually punched my spouse or physically harassed a coworker. If that's what you're thinking, I urge you to take a moment to read and really consider the words of the apostle James: "A tiny spark can set a great forest on fire. And the tongue is a flame of fire. It is a whole world of wickedness, corrupting your entire body. It can set your whole life on fire, for it is set on fire by hell itself" (James 3:5-6, NLT). James doesn't mince words, does he?

ONE THING

Begin seeing your words as a form of currency and resolve to "give away" at least one sincere compliment every day. An encouraging word from you may restore someone's hope or renew that person's confidence.

If you're a parent, are you aware of the profound effect your words have on your children? When I was in Albuquerque, New Mexico, for a speaking engagement, Donna and I were watching the Golf Channel on TV before it was time to head to the event. The program we were watching was profiling some of the greatest golfers, including Arnold Palmer. It showed pictures of him as a young boy. Then it focused on his win on the junior circuit before anyone knew the name Arnold Palmer. Now, at seventy-four, he remembered his father's reaction. He said that his father was more the stern type—not particularly encouraging. Yet with tears in his eyes, Arnold said he had won the tournament. Afterward, his dad came up to him and said, "I'm proud of you! Good job." Despite all the tournaments Palmer won after the junior circuit, isn't it interesting that he never forgot those words from his dad. Why? Because words matter. One thing you can do today to live intentionally is to remember the power of your words on other people.

After I spoke at a conference years ago, a young man came up to me and said, "When I was in college I ran track and I was good at what I did; in fact, I ran faster than anyone on the team. My dad was the firm type—few words, little encouragement. Instead, he would say, 'You can do better'—thinking he was encouraging me. I ran in a championship race and broke the school record! I ran faster than anyone had ever run that race and came across the finish line feeling good about what I had done. I turned to find my dad in the grandstands and saw him coming toward me. Instead of saying, 'Good job,' he yelled, 'You could have run faster.'"

Words are powerful. Maybe his dad was thinking, *You can do better, Son*, but what the son heard was, "You are not good enough." Words make a difference in people's lives. What was it you heard when your parents spoke to you as a child? What do your children or grandchildren hear when you speak to them?

ONE THING

With your spouse, decide when you can find at least a few minutes to talk one-on-one each day—perhaps as soon as you're both home or while walking the dog after dinner.

We must also watch what we say to other family members. If you have been married for more than a week or two, you have learned that words matter. When your wife comes up to you and says, "How does this look on me?" we guys need to watch out—this is a trick question. Get it wrong and you lose. Does she want the truth? Maybe, but be careful, because if you say, "Well, it doesn't look so good," she'll likely shoot back, "What's wrong with it?"

When I get up in the morning and I'm ready to go off to work, I always go through the inspection process. Donna is very gracious, but she will always check out how I am dressed to make sure it's okay. I've learned to walk out to the kitchen and present myself. Either she says, "Well, you look nice," which means I'm presentable, or "Are you going to wear that today?" which means I'm not. It's back to the bedroom for a change.

Once I found a sweater at the mall that I really liked. It was red with yellow stripes. When I had put it on and walked out of the dressing room, I asked Donna what she thought. From about fifty feet away, she yelled out, "They'll see you coming!" I got the message.

While I rely on Donna to be blunt when it comes to my wardrobe, I also know that she will not use words as a weapon to hurt me. Have you ever said something to someone you love that you wish you could take back? Have you ever hit the "send" button on an e-mail or on your mouth and then immediately wished you could pull it back? At that point, though, it's gone forever. You might like to "reel the baby back in," but it has already gotten off the hook.

One of the most-referenced Scripture verses when it comes to words is Proverbs 25:11: "A word aptly spoken is like apples of gold in settings of silver." Isn't that a beautiful word picture? The right word spoken at the right time can certainly change a life. And a cruel word can wreak havoc on our relationships.

WISE WORDS FROM KIDS

Our youngest son, Derek, is very creative; after college he studied at a Hollywood film institute hoping to use his talent in a positive way. Even when Derek was little, he made films. As Donna worked around the house, she would find props from his moviemaking adventures all over. He spent hours making a movie, and then Donna and I had to be the film critics. We even pitched in as extras or stars in his movies. Derek has always thought outside the box and has often spoken outside the box.

One night over dinner at a restaurant, Derek, who was about seven then, was deep in creative thought. All the while, he was making a mess with his food, moving it off the plate and here and there. Finally I said, "Derek, come on! We are out in a restaurant; knock it off! What is the problem? What is wrong with your food? It's all over the place!"

Derek looked across the table at me and said with all seriousness,

"You know, it must be that your food is calmer than mine!" Words. They can be funny, too.

I goofed around in elementary school, and when I was about to go into seventh grade, the school called my mother in. I wasn't a trouble-maker, but because I wasn't paying attention, I wasn't doing very well. The teacher told my mom, "Randy is a good kid, but when he goes to junior high we think we are going to put him in remedial classes." To me, this meant the class for dummies.

So in seventh grade I was in the remedial classes. All my friends carried blue math books, and I carried a green one. My friends all went down one hallway, and I had to go down another to my classroom. I remember thinking, *This is not going to last very long; I'm not hanging around this hallway. I'm going to get out of here.*

When I got into eighth grade, I started to discipline myself. A researcher from the University of Michigan came to our class and pulled us out for testing. When the researcher tested my verbal skills, she said, "When I give you a letter, tell me a word that comes to mind." She gave a letter and I answered with a word. She said *N* and I answered *name*. She said *K* and I answered *kite*.

She said the letter *P* and I wanted to show that I was not as dumb as they thought I was. I answered with the word *pneumonia*. She looked up and said, "What did you say?" I repeated, "Pneumonia."

She said, "That is really good!" (Apparently people in my class didn't normally come up with this kind of stuff.) I still remember her saying I had done well. I went back into the mainstream classes later in eighth grade and became an overachiever. When I went for my master's degree at the University of Arizona, I was determined to get a 4.0 and I did it. I then continued on to get my doctorate.

The researcher's words were powerful in my life. In just a few words, she told me I could do well. You can probably remember words spoken to you as a child or a student that changed your life—maybe some like these:

- You have a pretty smile; never quit smiling!
- You are a very kind person.

Conversely, maybe someone has told you something like this:

- You can do much better than that.
- You are never going to amount to anything.

Research shows that by the time the average twelfth grader graduates from high school, he or she will have been criticized many thousands of times. Perhaps you can remember people coming along when you were a kid who, by their discouraging words, blew out an ambition or dream, just as if they had extinguished a flickering candle. The words we say have power in our marriages, our families, the workplace, and the lives of our children. Your children will remember the words that you speak to them, and when they grow up, it's possible the words they remember you saying will be completely different from what you remember saying or how you intended to say to them.

UNINTENDED CONSEQUENCES

Have you ever said something you didn't think would offend someone but it did? One night as I drove up the driveway, I noticed a scrape all the way down the side of Donna's car. I walked into the kitchen where Donna was seated at the table and asked, "How did that happen?" And she responded, rightfully so, "I'm fine, thank you." While my first concern should have been for Donna, my question showed more concern for the car. My question had unintended consequences.

Sometimes our words have unintended consequences because they are interpreted differently by the listener than we intended. For the last couple of years, I've been threatening to write the *Carlson Dictionary of Marriage* explaining the misunderstood words used between husbands and wives. Here are a couple of examples:

ONE THING

Don't assume you have to take hurtful words to heart. Remember that words spoken by someone who is tired or in a hurry often come across differently than the speaker intended.

- *Shopping*: Women mean, "Let's walk around the mall and look at all the things the stores have." Men hear, "Let's go pick up that one item we need and come right back home."
- *Intimacy*: Women mean talking, hugging, sharing, holding hands. Men mean sexual intimacy.

Over the years, I've learned three ways to avoid unintended consequences of words:

- Before you speak, be clear on what you want to say.
- After you speak, be sure that what you said was understood. To do this, repeat what you said in another way to see if you were clear.
- Then be sure you understand the other person's response by asking, "I'm hearing you say _____. Is that right?"

TIMING IS EVERYTHING

Andrea, our only daughter and middle child, was preparing to go to the mission field in Outer Mongolia as I was starting to write this book. She is a godly young woman, and she has always been very determined and focused. When she took a high school placement test that recommended careers, she was told she'd make a good prison warden!

Because Andrea is so strong willed, she is the one child with whom I knocked heads. If I said something was black, she said it was white. If I said it was left, she said it was right. You get the picture. One thing I learned was that timing was important when communicating with Andrea.

When Andrea was a little girl she never felt like I really listened to her (and this is something I have to work on even today, now that we're both adults). I guess as a dad, I had my mind in other places at times. I grew up with guys, so I didn't understand that she wanted to talk. I asked our sons questions like, "How was your day?" ("Fine") or "Is anything wrong?" ("Nope"), and that level of communication seemed to suffice for them.

But when I asked Andrea about her day, I heard all about it—her friends, her teachers, and what happened at lunch. Apparently I was not a very good listener, so one night when she was about ten, she sat at the kitchen table and said, "You never listen to me!" She got up and stomped down the hall.

Of course, I jumped up and said, "Young lady, you don't talk to me that way." As I headed down the hall to set her straight, I looked over my shoulder at Donna, who was wearing the look that says, "I wouldn't do that if I were you. If you want to be a smart father you should turn around and come back here and sit down."

But I continued to Andrea's room and found her lying on the bed, sobbing. God spoke to me very clearly at that point. And instead of getting on her case, I got down on my knees and said to her, "You know, Andrea, you are right! I've never been a daddy to a daughter before, and I'm learning with you. Will you forgive me?"

> ## ONE THING
>
> When one of your kids asks to talk, make it a point to make yourself available as soon as possible. Then really listen—turn your back to the computer, turn off the TV, and turn your full attention onto your child.

The timing wasn't right to set her straight by saying, "I'm the dad and I'm in charge." The timing was right to let her know that, as a dad, I had blown it.

Timing in a relationship is essential when it comes to the words we speak. Mark Twain said, "The right word may be effective, but no word was ever as effective as a rightly timed pause."

The right word at the wrong time creates confusion, as does the wrong word at the right time. The right word at the right time sparks encouragement.

Check Your Timing before You Speak

If you sometimes regret what you say, stop a moment before opening your mouth. Ask yourself, *Is what I'm about to say in the best interest of the other person or the best way to build the relationship?* So often we speak because we want to get something off our chests, and we don't consider whether our words are in the best interest of the other person.

Then consider whether the person you're about to speak to is mature enough to receive what you need to say. You might be telling the truth, and it might need to be said at some point, but the truth must be spoken in love only when the person can understand and handle what you say.

Think twice or even three times before you speak. The carpenter's motto, "Measure twice and cut once," can be applied to our words. Think twice and speak once. What often happens is that we end up having to speak several times to get it straight because we didn't think it through beforehand.

Here's one thing you could start doing today that could immediately improve a relationship: start thinking twice before you speak, by asking yourself the following three questions:

- What needs to be said and why?
- How should I say it so that it will be understood and received as I intend it?
- When should I say it? What would be the best time to bring this up?

Thomas learned the hard way that words wound. His angry, blaming words cost him his wife, children, and job. Of course, he could have responded to Maria's early objections to his words by apologizing, by going to God and asking for help, or by going to counseling for his anger. The relationship probably could have been healed if he had stopped his destructive verbal attacks early on. Sadly, he learned about the power of his words too late to save his marriage. If words are damaging your relationships, you don't have to make the same mistake. What one small thing can you begin doing so that you speak only life-giving words?

ONE THING

Before correcting or confronting someone about his or her behavior or attitude, ask yourself, *Is this the right time and place to discuss this?* Then ask, *How can I say this so it builds this person up rather than tearing him or her down?*

ONE SMALL THING TO BEGIN CHANGING YOUR LIFE

■ Here's another "one thing" you could do today. Make a list of the phrases you use that need to be eliminated from your speech, such as:

— "You never . . ." Everybody does something right once in a while.

— "You always . . ." Focus on the here and now, not the past and future.

— "Why don't you . . . ?" This is a quiet but hurtful way of expressing your disapproval or comparing a person to someone else. ("Why don't you get good grades like your brother?")

— "I hate you." These words can destroy a relationship permanently.

— "I don't want to talk about it." These words leave no room for discussion and growth.

— Other: _____

■ Eliminate one unhealthy or unnecessary word or phrase from your vocabulary starting today and watch what happens.

■ Add one new healthy phrase at a time to your vocabulary until it becomes a new habit, such as:

— "I love you."

— "I'm proud of you."

— "Good job."

— "Tell me more."

— "You've worked hard on that."

— "You can do it."

— "How can I help you?"

9
The Power of One Thing to Change How You Use Your Time

The great dividing line between success and failure can be expressed in five words: I did not have time.
—Franklin Field, British politician

Raj, an information services manager, arrives at work every day at 7 a.m. After buying coffee in the office cafeteria, he heads upstairs to his third-floor cubicle. He looks forward to thirty uninterrupted minutes to sip his coffee while reading the newspaper he brings from home. He usually waits until 7:30 to open his e-mail.

One Wednesday, however, he decided just to see what had happened overnight and glanced at his in-box. Seventy-two messages had arrived since he logged off the day before at 5:30 p.m. The number of e-mails didn't faze him. Because Raj participated in several office committees and served two internal clients, he was copied on dozens of e-mails every day.

It was the message with the red exclamation point from the company's chief technology officer that caught—or grabbed—his attention immediately. "Raj, the system was down all night and I had four calls at home between 2 and 4 a.m. Can you please look into this and be sure we don't have a repeat performance tonight? I meet with the press at 9 tomorrow, and I'd hate to be up all night troubleshooting."

Raj's plans for the day quickly flew out the window. He had planned to meet with two employees who had leadership potential to discuss their personal development plans. A new software vendor, who had a product Raj believed could improve the company's reliability, was also scheduled to make a presentation to his team.

He sent a text message to his administrative assistant, asking him to clear his calendar so he could put out this fire that had burst into flame during the night.

How often does that happen to you—you wake up with great plans for the day, only to find yourself pulled into other activities that suddenly seem more urgent? That's not necessarily a bad thing—after all, Raj simply determined that responding to his boss's request was more important than his own plans.

If you live to be seventy-five, you will have about twenty-seven thousand days of life. Since you are an adult, the days and the hours of those days are under your control. You decide what to do with them, for better or worse.

ONE THING

When blocking out time for the priorities on your daily schedule, build in an extra thirty minutes for the most important tasks. Most projects take longer than anticipated.

It's interesting to contrast our view of time with God's view of eternity. In the song "The Line Between the Two," Mark Harris offers the reminder that there will be two dates on your tombstone—the day you were born and the day you will die—but you live your life in that little line between the two. Life is short, especially when viewed in the light of eternity. In Psalm 90:12 (NKJV) we read, "Teach us to number our days, that we may gain a heart of wisdom." If we are going to be smart in how we use that little line between the two dates of our lives, we need wisdom that can come only from God.

God, of course, is the timekeeper of our lives. He starts the timer and then, usually many years later, he stops it. I recall vividly the occasions when he started the timer for each of our children's lives. Because Donna and I had been married eight years by the time our first child, Evan, was born, I felt we were focused and ready to go that first time in the delivery room. I knew God had ordained the beginning of his life, and I had the same assurance when Andrea and Derek were born.

To make the most of that little line in between your beginning and ending dates, you must view your calendar as your autobiography. If I were to look at your calendar and what you do each day, I would be able to see how you use your time and what is important to you.

Do you ever look back at your calendar and think about how you used your time? I make it a practice on the first day of every year to go back through my calendar from the year just ended and ask myself, *Was I intentional with the use of my time?*

Time is lived in the present with a view toward the future, but it's understood as we look to the past. Solomon is an example of the wisdom gained from years of life and reflection. According to some scholars, he wrote Song of Solomon, a picture of passion, in his youth; and he wrote Proverbs in his middle years, by which time he had gained much wisdom. But not until the book of Ecclesiastes do we see the great wisdom Solomon attained through age. At this point of his life, what he saw was through the rearview mirror—his life was behind him. Ecclesiastes 12:13 sums it up beautifully: "Fear God and keep his commandments, for this is the whole duty of man."

That is wisdom—fear God and do what he says. That is intentional living. But how do we do this when it comes to spending our time? The American Time Use Survey collected information about what people spend time on each day, and here's what it found for Americans age fifteen or older:

- 8.6 hours sleeping
- 5.1 hours doing leisure and/or sport activities
- 3.7 hours working (remember, this survey includes ages fifteen and above and is an average of all days of the week)
- 4.7 hours participating in a variety of activities including eating, drinking, going to school, and shopping

Do you see anything missing? What I don't see is time spent on life's essentials, such as relationships, time with God, and personal growth. We spend most of our time on routine activities that don't help us achieve our goals and dreams.

I find that people, myself included, spend a lot of time putting out fires—urgent matters that demand our immediate attention—as when Raj had to scrap his plans for the day to address a computer crisis.

Raj put out the fire, but it meant putting off other important things; namely, meeting with key employees and a new vendor. The urgent presented itself, and what was important suffered. This happens at home as well. So many things need to get done each day—household chores, homework, bills, meals—that we often flop into bed without having had time to read our Bibles or spend much time talking with our children or spouses.

Successful people are intentional about how they use their time. They know their priorities, and when they are faced with an emergency or unavoidable interruption, they do what needs to be done and then get right back on track. Yes, they are busy, but they also understand the value of rest and have learned the importance of setting aside time to rejuvenate. Surprisingly, unsuccessful people may also be quite busy. The difference is that they are far less likely to know where they're headed or even why they're doing something. They easily succumb to avoidable distractions.

What about you? How well do you use your time? Take this little yes-or-no quiz to see if you are using time effectively to achieve what you want to achieve.

1. At the end of most days, do you feel as if you focused on your priorities, or do you think you allowed less important things to distract you?
2. Are you less focused than you want to be on the important things in your life?
3. Do you procrastinate instead of completing important tasks in a timely way?
4. Are you frustrated with the way you use your time?

If you answered yes to any of these questions, you need to be more intentional in the use of your time. (This is an area where I struggle too.) After all, time is an important God-given gift. We need to manage it as stewards, just as we manage our money, our health, our environment, and our relationships.

How to Waste Time

Ephesians 5:11 (*The Message*) says, "Don't waste your time on useless work, mere busywork, the barren pursuits of darkness." Here are some time wasters that can really eat up this precious asset:

1. **Procrastinating.** One reason deadlines help many of us is that they get us focused when we know our time is almost up. The night before your final exam in high school or college was probably a night of intense focus and work. Of course, the all-nighter didn't produce the results that solid study and preparation throughout the semester would have produced, but desperation certainly energized you, right?

   Perfectionism can also cause procrastination. Simone was a perfectionist with a very messy house. Though she hated living in such chaos, she said, "I know I'm not going to be able to keep it perfect, so I can't even try. It would be too frustrating to keep trying and trying to get it right."

   Don't focus on perfection unless perfection is necessary, as it is for the heart surgeon performing a lifesaving procedure. Far too many of us bog down either in the vicious cycle of perfectionism or in our desire to give up because we feel like hopeless failures.

   Instead, focus on completion. If a task will take less than three minutes to do and it needs to get done, do it now! Think of all the little unfinished tasks that are causing you to feel overwhelmed and discouraged, such as writing a note, paying a bill, calling a friend, solving a problem, fixing a leaky faucet, or in Simone's case, hanging up the clothes piled on a chair in her bedroom. Take care of one of those things now!

   ONE THING

   First thing each day, decide on the single most important thing you must do—whether a phone call, a bill to pay, a job application to submit, or prayer for your spouse or children. At the first opportunity, do it.

2. **Staying busy doing the wrong things.** Busyness is not evidence of progress or accomplishment. Neither is exhaustion. Accomplishment is measured by results, not frenetic activity. That's the problem with many committees: members can talk for hours but produce little. As comedian Milton Berle said, "A committee is a group that keeps minutes and loses hours."

3. **Thinking too much about other people.** It's good to care enough about others to think about how you can pray for them or serve them. But when we simply wonder what they are doing, what they think of us, what they should be doing, or how they should change their lives, we're just wasting time. When callers to my radio program ask me how they can get someone to act differently, I tell them, "You can't change someone else—you can only change yourself. Get focused on your own life, be what God wants you to be, pray for this person, ask God to move in his or her life, and hold that person accountable, if necessary." Trying to change someone else keeps us from much more productive activities.

4. **Worrying.** When you worry, you freeze. You're not really living in the present; instead, you're either regretting what happened in the past or dreading what might happen in the future. It's hard to be productive when you're worrying, and it can lead to procrastination, guilt, and feelings of failure.

5. **Oversleeping.** No explanation needed. Get up and get going every day!

6. **Searching for lost items.** This is a time waster for me. While walking through our house, I'll sometimes take my glasses off and set them down on the counter, the bed, or the table. Often I forget where I put them. I'm so blind without glasses that I have to call out, "Donna, where are my glasses?"

    Likewise, clutter—whether it's in our closets, our garage, our minds, or our emotions—leads us to waste a lot of time searching for things. (If clutter is an issue for you, see chapter 11 for more tips on dealing with this time waster.)

7. **Being indecisive.** Continually going over a situation trying to make the perfect decision is sometimes a waste of time. A caller to our program said, "I've been praying about this and praying about this," and it was so obvious what she ought to be doing. I told her there is a point when you have to stop praying about it and just do what you know you need to do! It's important to pray and wait on God, but sometimes we avoid making a decision by saying we are still praying about it, even when we know deep down what we should do.

ONE THING

Journal your worries into prayers.

Do any of these time wasters apply to you? You may be able to think of others, like checking e-mail too often, engaging in long and unnecessary phone conversations, or hunting for addresses or phone numbers you should keep handy. I know I sometimes struggle to use my time wisely. But I am—and you can be—determined to use time more deliberately.

SPEND OR INVEST?

When asked, "How can you write so many books?" Chuck Swindoll said he gets up an hour earlier than everybody else to do nothing but write. Think of it: one hour each day times six days each week times fifty-two weeks each year is 312 hours each year. You, too, could write a book in 312 hours—or accomplish something else that is important to you.

The key to being intentional about time is to understand that you have the power to *use* or *invest* your time, not just *spend* it. Money used and invested wisely is more likely to grow into something valuable than money we recklessly spend. Think of time the same way. Invest it well rather than wasting it.

Since time fills up with something—or nothing—depending on how we use or invest it, you must be deliberate in your use of time to be successful. I'm not suggesting that you start planning each minute for maximum use or that you go up on top of a mountain and just think twenty-four hours each day. But start with thirty minutes. Today try this one thing—set aside thirty minutes to concentrate on one of the most important, but neglected, areas of your life and then tell me how that felt (go to www.TheIntentionalLife.com). Here are some places to find those thirty minutes:

- Shut off the television for thirty minutes.
- Shorten the time you spend on Facebook or Twitter by thirty minutes.
- Refuse to spend any time today in gossip.
- Get up thirty minutes earlier.
- Stay up thirty minutes later tonight.

If you reinvest thirty minutes daily in one of these easy ways, over a year you will add four and a half workweeks, or 182 hours, to your life. Imagine having eight hours a day for four weeks that you could focus on the most important things in your life.

One good way to invest your newfound thirty minutes would be to use it to think through the issues you identified in your thinking list in chapter 5. Or you could use fifteen minutes for that and fifteen minutes to begin one of the action steps at the end of this chapter.

Our use of time is a critical factor in whether we will be successful or unsuccessful in the important areas of life. Successful people keep the main thing the main thing. They don't let their time fill up with busyness that keeps them from the important parts of their lives that really need attention.

A Chinese proverb says, "One cannot manage too many affairs—like pumpkins in the water, one pops up while you try to hold down the other." Sometimes we stay busy holding down pumpkins—letting our time fill up with inconsequential things—until something else pops up to demand our attention. Many people spend their time doing lots of less important things.

When we know that Christ is our main thing and that our purpose in life is to honor him, we can focus on that main thing. We all have different talents and abilities, but our purpose is always to know, love, and honor God.

For many mothers with kids at home, parenting is the one thing in their current season of life. Yet I often talk to moms who have decided to stay home with their children, only to fill their lives with a thousand other things that distract them from the very thing they wanted to do—be there to raise those kids. Whatever is your main thing right now needs to be your primary focus.

Successful people barter their time for fewer right things; other people barter their time for lots of different things. I've noticed that when I'm focused on a few things of great value, I am more productive and get more in return than when I give away ten minutes here, fifteen minutes there, and two minutes someplace else.

Until we set aside time in our days when we cannot be interrupted, even for "urgent" matters, we will continue sacrificing needed attention to what is most important. After all, when people say a matter is "urgent," they may just mean, "I want it done now."

Some families determine that the dinner hour is sacrosanct—no phone calls, text messages, people at the door, or any other interruption will be permitted to violate this time.

At work, it may be hard to say no to a supervisor, but it may be possible to block off time on your calendar to use for what is truly important. When an urgent need presents itself during that time, you can say, "I have an important client meeting in a half hour, but I will start on the presentation after that."

ONE THING

Schedule your most important tasks at the time of day when you have the most energy and think the clearest.

The day Raj was asked to address the computer problem was a long one. He wasn't able to leave the office until ten that night, even though he'd thought he resolved the issue in time to make his daughter's piano recital earlier that evening. First thing that morning, he had assembled a virtual team with technologists from around the world who had analyzed and solved the server problem. The coding changes had been made, the application had been tested, and the server had been up and running for three hours by 5 p.m. As Raj was packing his briefcase, the phone rang and he picked it up. One of the troubleshooting technicians apologized profusely but informed Raj that the system had crashed again. The process would have to start all over.

This urgent situation meant that Raj missed something important—very important—his daughter's recital. His family's disappointment was another consequence of putting out this fire. Raj knew he had to do something so that these fires didn't burn up his relationships with the people he valued most.

I know how hard this can be. Today, for example, I had scheduled to hide myself away so I could finish this section of the book—no distractions, please. In large part I succeeded, but because some of my staff knew I was hiding out somewhere in the building, they hunted me down. With apologies, they told me, "It will only take a minute" or "Just give me a quick call when you take a break" or "You're the only one who can decide this." It's ego building to be made to feel so important! Yet it's a time killer to what's more important. So, in addition to writing, I met individually with some of our leadership team to provide additional direction and spent time encouraging my staff. But the one thing that will make this day the most intentional is for me to stay on task and finish this section of the book.

It's really a matter of self-discipline. I have to hold myself and others accountable to my calendar if I hope to use my time effectively. I've learned that I can't manage time—I can only manage myself. Either I control my schedule or my life is out of control. This is a lesson Raj still needs to learn. The important matters that could have significantly improved his organization had to be shelved when the fire alarm sounded. Looking back, Raj feels he had no choice but to devote his entire day to that crisis. Perhaps in this case he was right. Yet he must be

> *I've learned that I can't manage time—I can only manage myself.*

careful. We can't control emergencies, but we can make sure that only the big fires disrupt our schedules.

ONE SMALL THING TO BEGIN CHANGING YOUR LIFE

- Making sure you have your important "one thing" on your list, schedule each hour of tomorrow in advance, leaving no gaps where time wasters can sneak in. If you want to do something fun, even something that might be considered a waste of time, go for it—but make sure you schedule it.

- Get out your calendar or BlackBerry and review the last three months. Do you approve of how you spent your time? What value did you derive from the way you spent your time? Which events or activities produced little value?

- Look ahead on your calendar and write down all the "main thing dates" for the next twelve months. A year from now, what events or activities would you would like to see on your calendar? What main things on your calendar would indicate that you had used your time wisely and accomplished what's most important to you?

10
THE POWER OF ONE THING TO CHANGE HOW YOU PICK FRIENDS

My best friend is the one who brings out the best in me.
—HENRY FORD

Scott had many friends—people were naturally drawn to him. But he was closest to a small group of men whom he really trusted. These men formed an accountability group. They met regularly to learn from one another and keep one another on the right track. Scott shared his life with this group of men—his hopes, dreams, struggles, and challenges. He was devoted to these guys, and he believed the feeling was mutual. But one of them betrayed him by sharing a confidence Scott had asked the group not to share. The confidence concerned a problem in Scott's family, and it got back to Scott's wife, Sherry, in a roundabout way. She was devastated.

As you may know from personal experience, investing and trusting in a friendship make us vulnerable, and we can be hurt. But friendship is worth the risk. Friends add richness and zest to our lives, and they often encourage and challenge us in invaluable ways.

I define friendship as a growing relationship built on love, honesty, trust, mutual respect, and shared interests and values between two equally mature people who have no hidden agendas or desires to control each other. On my radio program, when people call and tell me that a friend has hurt them, I always say, "You'd better define the nature of your relationship and understand what that relationship is. Is it really a friendship? You can avoid most misunderstandings and broken relationships if care is given to the expectations you and your friend have for each other."

Friendships are enriching experiences, but they can also cause pain. In this chapter I want to help you assess your friendships and their health. Then I'd like you to decide one thing you can do to improve your friendships and your choice of friends in the future.

A Crucial Choice

The friends you choose to let into your life will either build you up and encourage you to a higher level of success, or they will pull you down to their level of immaturity and discouragement. The choice of friends is yours, so choose carefully.

We all have those whom we call, or who call themselves, our friends. We use the word *friend* like we use the word *love*. I love pizza, but I *love* Donna. We have lots of friends, but then we have *friends* at a much deeper level, people with whom we're honest and vulnerable, those whose thinking influences our thinking about life. This is the kind of friendship I'm talking about in this chapter.

Successful people are intentional about their friendships. They seek out positive people who will help them grow in their walk with God. They may have many acquaintances but just a handful of close friends. Other people "need" friends, even if they drain them of energy or influence them negatively. They may have dozens of "friends," none of whom know them deeply.

ONE THING

Seek out a mentor at church, in your neighborhood, or in your workplace who can help you develop your interpersonal skills.

Has a friend—someone you thought you could trust—ever done you wrong? If so, you probably felt as if you had been knifed in the back or had your legs cut out from underneath you, because you never saw it coming. You expected much more from this person than he or she delivered.

We know that friendship is essential to a healthy, successful life. But many times we allow people to be our friends by default—just because they're there and we're here and circumstances throw us together. Someone expresses a desire to spend time with us, and a "friendship" is born. But not everyone is a good friend for us.

In Proverbs 17:17 (NLT) we read, "A friend is always loyal, and a brother is born to help in time of need." This verse describes a true friend. Let's look at some characteristics of both healthy and unhealthy friendships.

Traits of a healthy friendship

1. Friends love and influence each other, but they don't control each other.
2. Friends are honest with each other without fear of rejection or retaliation.
3. Friends respect each other enough to speak the truth—to be who they really are and, at times, to hold each other accountable. Friends sometimes have to love each other enough to challenge the other to stop doing something that is destructive or harmful.
4. Friends don't manipulate or play games to get their way.
5. Friends don't have anything to gain from the friendship (besides the joy of the friendship).
6. Friends have some shared values.

As you can see, the give-and-take in a healthy friendship is mutual and respectful. But what are the signs that you're in an unhealthy friendship?

Signs of an unhealthy friendship

1. You feel like you need to walk on eggshells when you're around your friend. You're careful about what you say so you don't offend him or her.
2. You hold back because you're not sure you can trust this person. You wonder if what you say will be turned against you.
3. When you fail, instead of feeling encouragement from this person, you feel judged or as if he or she is almost happy about your setback.
4. When you succeed, this person isn't as thrilled for you as you expected.

As you've read these indicators of both healthy and unhealthy friendships, did anyone come to mind? Or do these symptoms make you think perhaps you are the weak person in a friendship? Do you control the friendship in an unhealthy way? Are you trustworthy so your friends know you will keep a confidence? Do you feel a sense of competition or the need to be the best in a group?

Let's talk about some principles that will help you assess and understand your friendships and the kind of friend you are to others.

THE WEAK LINK

The weakest person in a friendship controls the relationship. Just as a chain breaks at its weakest link, so the weaker member of a friendship determines its strength. When stress is applied, the link between the two people breaks. Have you ever gotten together with a group of friends and noticed that one person was controlling the gathering? He or she was domineering, manipulative, or overly sensitive (or some combination of these), and you couldn't quite trust that what you said wouldn't be misunderstood or repeated. Have you ever been in a group and realized you're cautious about one person there? You've likely discovered the weakest link in that group.

Friendships are important, so choose them carefully.

Are all "friends" friends?

I don't believe that all "friends" should be defined as friends, including those you work with, people you mentor or those who mentor you, teachers, and parents.

At work you relate with other people on a mission, vision, or responsibility, so you're friends in the sense that you work together and support each other. But deep, intimate, vulnerable sharing with another person is difficult in the workplace. Why? First, you can't share your weaknesses or be totally honest because you fear these shortcomings could be used against you. Second, you probably see your coworkers only at work and don't get the opportunity to connect at a deeper level.

Think about what sometimes happens when friends become business partners. Suddenly the dynamics or the expectations of the relationship begin to change. When money is involved, both partners want more control, especially when some of that money is theirs. They may be disappointed if they discover that their partner's business ability or work ethic isn't as great as they'd thought. Just as many work relationships aren't really friendships, when we take a friendship and try to put it into another place or situation, it may not work either.

Mentoring, guiding, and caring for someone involves people at different levels of maturity and experience. For that reason, this kind of interaction is more of a teaching relationship than a close friendship. Teachers may be friendly to students, but they can't be a peer. They're in a position of authority, not friendship.

And parents can't truly be their children's friends until they no longer have authority over them. Only when your children grow up and are making their own decisions can you be friends. Until then, your child needs you as a parent, not a buddy.

ONE THING

Don't respond to your children as friends but as their parents. For instance, if they need your discipline, ask yourself, *What is best for them?* not, *Will they be mad at me if I do this?*

I tell parents who try to be their child's best friend, "You're the only person on earth who can be your child's mom or dad. She needs you to have a backbone and stand up as a parent for what is right." My son Evan and I are now good friends. That's possible because I no longer have authority over him. He and his wife decide how to raise their family, and as grandparents Donna and I stand back and cheer them on.

Best if used by 2010?

Many things, such as milk, medicine, and batteries, have an expiration date—a time when it's no longer safe to use them or keep them around. Some friendships also need to have an expiration date. If you hang on to a close friendship beyond its natural expiration date, it may sour and become distasteful to one or both parties. This may sound like a new concept—am I saying some friendships should actually come to an end? Yes, sometimes friends need to move on.

1. **Experiential friendships.** Remember when you went to camp as a kid? While sharing a bunk bed in a cabin, you and another kid became best friends. By the end of the week you were sure you were best friends for life. You'd been around the campfire and shared the deep secrets that only twelve-year-olds can share. You went home and wrote a letter to your new best friend. He or she wrote back once, and then you never heard from the person again.

   We all have formed friendships based on a shared experience that came to an end. We connected because of the experience for a period of time, but the friendship expired. One person might have wanted to hang on, but the other person said, "Camp is over, and I'm going on with my life."

2. **Phase-of-life friendships.** When I was a kid growing up in a suburb of Detroit, both my brothers were amateur radio operators. Eventually I got a ham license too, and we did Morse code and talked to people around the country. My buddy Bob, who lived behind our house, was my best friend. He also caught on to amateur radio and got his ham license. We'd get up late at night and go into his or my room, turn down the lights, and turn on the radio with those tubes that glowed, heated up the room, and brought in a signal from somewhere in the world. We'd find a signal—a Morse code—coming in and would wait to hear the senders' call letters. Once we had that, we knew where in the world they were located. Then we'd send back our signal and start to talk to each other.

   This may sound silly in an age of cell phones and text messaging, but Bob and I were really connected around amateur radio. But then my family moved to another part of the city, and I haven't talked to Bob since. Our friendship was part of the phase of life when two boys share a hobby; in our case, talking to people all over the world and then putting pins on the map to show where the people were.

3. **Need-based friendships.** Two moms who are new to a community might connect and become friends as they try to establish them-

selves. The friendship serves a purpose for a time, but sometimes the deep connections needed for a lasting friendship aren't there.

Some friendships have expiration dates, and that's not bad or wrong. In fact, I think some of us have friends we're hanging around with whom we've grown beyond spiritually. We love them and encourage them, but instead of lifting us up, they bring us down.

ONE THING

Before giving in to a demanding friend's request, make a point of talking to your spouse (or, if you're single, a trusted friend) to get another person's perspective on what is reasonable.

If you hang on to a friendship after its expiration, it may spoil or become ineffective, just like food or medicine past its expiration date. If you want to grow, be around people who are growing. If you want to get stronger, be around people who are stronger than you are. If you want to become more spiritual, be around people who will encourage spiritual development.

Of course, even good friends occasionally have conflict. So how do you know when it's time to end a friendship?

1. You use caller ID to avoid talking to this person.
2. Given a choice today, you wouldn't pick that person to be your friend again.
3. You feel drained after spending time together.
4. You feel obligated to spend time with this person.
5. You feel controlled by him or her.
6. You feel used or taken advantage of—this person is always asking for something.
7. You're starting to pull away and find excuses not to be together.
8. You're losing respect for him or her.
9. You're losing trust in him or her.
10. You no longer share the same values.
11. You've outgrown this person.

Dangerous liaisons

The research is clear—the best marriages occur when friends marry. My very best friend on the face of the earth is my wife, Donna. She is one person I can talk to about anything. In fact, I talk so much after getting into bed that I often put her to sleep. She claims it's my calming voice. But I know I can share anything with her. Friendship is the core of a solid marriage relationship, though obviously marriage has an added dimension of intimacy.

My relationship with Donna is so tight, so close, so intimate that when I have things I want to share, she's the one I logically and naturally go to. I don't need to share with anyone else of the opposite sex.

Married people who have opposite-sex friendships with people other than their spouses may be asking for trouble. I devoted an entire chapter to the topic of opposite-sex friendships in my book *Starved for Affection*. I talked about the power of opposite-sex friendships and how they can be very destructive. Let me share just seven of the twenty questions created by psychologist Dr. Todd Linaman that I included in that book—questions we need to ask ourselves about any relationship with a person of the opposite sex outside of our marriage. (You can see the entire list in the book or at www.TheIntentionalLife.com.) If you have such a relationship, how would you answer these questions?

1. Is your spouse unaware of your opposite-sex friendship? Maybe you aren't consciously trying to be secretive, but you're aware that you have a friendship that your spouse doesn't know anything about. That's a giant red flag.
2. Would you behave differently around your friend if your spouse were present? We can have friends in the workplace, in church, or elsewhere—but if you find yourself acting differently when your spouse shows up, you need to take that as a warning sign. If you are married and can't be yourself at all times with a person of the opposite sex, then you've got a problem.
3. Are you physically or emotionally attracted to your friend? Huge red flag!
4. Do you ever compare your spouse to your friend? You wouldn't do

it overtly, but you think, *Why can't my spouse be like that?* Your friend may not even know this is going on.

5. Does your friend fulfill needs, such as connecting emotionally, spending time together, or listening to you, that you wish your spouse would meet?
6. Do you and your friend ever exchange highly personal details about your lives or complain about your marriages to each other?
7. If your spouse does know about this friendship, has he or she ever expressed concern about your friendship with this person?

If you answer yes to any of these seven questions, you've been warned. You're on a dangerous path, and you've got problems ahead. I've been in the business of helping people for a long time, and I can tell you that no one starts on this path thinking it's going to lead to an affair or disrupt his or her marriage. But time after time, I've seen these friendships cross the line.

Fix It or Finish It

It's hard to end a friendship, but if you're developing an unhealthy friendship, it's imperative that you do. Sometimes a friendship just fades away. At other times the most loving thing you can do is say, "We don't share the same values anymore. While I want to continue to be your friend, we're going to have a new kind of relationship." You might get a negative reaction, but if this has been a strong relationship, it's valuable to honestly express your feelings and what you see as differences between you.

Sometimes you can figure out a new way to relate to each other that will meet each of your needs. Perhaps you can honestly say, "I'm not comfortable in our relationship anymore because of _____. I'm not willing to be around that kind of behavior [or conversation or activity], but I'll gladly work with you to find help if you want to change."

I'm not suggesting you stop caring about, praying for, or reaching out to a friend; I'm simply saying that if you're no longer headed in the same direction, you must redefine the relationship you have. You will no longer expect things you might get from a close relationship. Even if you sometimes feel used, you may be willing to continue connecting with this person because you want to reach him or her for the Lord. If you don't define the nature of the relationship, however, you may get yourself into trouble.

Choosing Friends

Not every person should have permission to be in your life, particularly the inner sanctum of your life. Not every person who wants to be your friend should be your friend. Samuel Johnston said, "True happiness consists not in the multitude of friends, but in their worth and choice."

I'm very careful about whom I choose to hang around because I know that I influence them and they influence me. It goes both ways. Just as not everyone is good for you, you aren't good for every person. You might have struggles or issues that could influence someone in the wrong direction. Maybe you tend to be critical, and a young or immature friend might pick up your negative ways.

Jesus had lots of friends. He was a friend to sinners, the Scripture says, in the sense of ministering to or caring for people. But his most intimate friends were his disciples. We all need that kind of deep friendship.

Make sure you're comfortable with the people you've let into your life. You should be able to be your real self and relax around them. Ralph Waldo Emerson said, "It is one of the blessings of old friends that you can afford to be stupid with them." That's a definition of a great friendship—I can be stupid and my friend will still love me!

ONE THING

If you're new to town or just want to make new friendships, intentionally seek out a book club, sports league, or class where you're likely to meet others with similar interests and values.

Make sure you don't need each other to be okay—neediness is not friendship. Your attitude should be: I'm okay with you; I'm okay without you, but I want to be a part of your life and both of us are better as a result of our friendship.

Will you both be better people as a result of your friendship? Do you add to each other or subtract from each other? Proverbs 27:10 (NLT) says, "Never abandon a friend—either yours or your father's. When disaster strikes, you won't have to ask your brother for assistance. It's better to go to a neighbor than to a brother who lives far away."

HONESTY: THE BEST POLICY IN A FRIENDSHIP

After Scott's close friend betrayed him by sharing a confidence, Scott was tempted to keep his deepest struggles and thoughts to himself. *I'll never let that happen to me or Sherry again,* he thought. But when he talked it over with his wife, she wisely suggested that instead of no longer talking openly with this group of friends, he sit down and talk to the one who had broken his trust, explaining the hurt that had resulted.

Do you have a friend who will challenge you when you need to be challenged? Someone who will step up and say, "You're out of line. I love you enough to challenge you"? You know, there are men who would not have cheated on their wives if a friend had stepped up and asked, "Are you being faithful to your wife?" or said, "I see something in your life that I'm concerned about." That's what friends are about. True friends are willing to confront in a loving way because they're trusted—they have that level of depth in the relationship.

Has a particular friend gotten you down? Are you worried that this person may be a bad influence or is intruding in uncomfortable ways? If so, begin doing one thing today to assess your relationship. Then prayerfully decide what, if any, action you need to take. And if you are now convicted that you are the source of the problem in a friendship that is important to you, begin doing one thing today to turn things around.

ONE SMALL THING TO BEGIN CHANGING YOUR LIFE

- List your closest friends. Then ask yourself the following questions about the first person on your list. Write down your answers.
  — Does this friendship fit the true definition of a healthy friendship (exhibits honesty, respect, accountability, shared values, no manipulation)?

— Does this person inspire or discourage you?

— Do either of you have a hidden agenda in the relationship (something one of you wants to get out of it besides friendship)?

— What would make the relationship better (e.g., more honesty, less anger, more respect)?

— What could you say in a loving, direct conversation that would let your friend know how you feel? Pray about it and then do it this week.

■ Repeat the process for each additional person on your list.

■ Ask yourself, *Do I need to take any steps to fix or improve any of these relationships?* If the answer is yes, pray about how you will go about it, plan how you will do it, and take action.

11
THE POWER OF ONE THING TO UNCLUTTER YOUR LIFE

Three rules of work: out of clutter find simplicity; from discord find harmony; in the middle of difficulty lies opportunity.

—ALBERT EINSTEIN

When eighty-year-old Doris died, no one knew about it for more than a week. She was a private person, according to her neighbors, with few visitors—actually *no* visitors that anyone could remember. When Sam, her next-door neighbor, saw the newspapers and mail piling up on her front porch, he debated whether to knock on the door to see if she was all right. *Maybe she went on a trip,* he thought. With a nagging conscience, Sam waited a few more days before approaching the mail carrier as she arrived with his mail.

"I don't know Doris next door very well—she keeps to herself—but I wonder about all the mail and papers that are piling up."

The mail carrier said that unless a stop is put on someone's house, mail is delivered every day until it becomes obvious that no one is collecting the mail. Then subsequent mail is held at the post office to be picked up.

Sam didn't know any of Doris's relatives, so after knocking on her front door numerous times, he called the police, who found her dead inside the house. Besides the accumulation of mail and newspapers on the front porch, police found piles of papers and magazines, empty egg cartons and milk containers, and unopened packages that Doris had apparently ordered by phone in response to TV ads. The only place the floor was visible was a narrow path from her recliner to the television, which was still turned on. When the police arrived, an infomercial that might have persuaded Doris to order one more thing for her useless collection was playing in the background.

The neighbors got a glimpse inside as Doris was removed from her home while one of the officers asked if anyone knew of a relative they could contact. No one knew of any.

The authorities finally tracked down an adult son who admitted he hadn't talked with his mother for several months. Apparently she was a bitter woman who'd never forgiven her ex-husband for walking out on her. Every time her son called, she would talk about nothing except how much she hated his father. Eventually she pushed her only child away.

A Place for Everything

Clutter can be a sign of an out-of-control, miserable life. Doris's home and heart were filled with clutter. Just as the papers and garbage made her home unsightly, so the bitterness and anger in her heart repelled other people.

While we may not be drowning in clutter like Doris, we may still have clutter in our lives that is diverting us from our priorities. Our garages and closets may be chock-full of all sorts of junk. We may have bags of clothes we have outgrown, boxes of knickknacks, and piles of paper. But not all the clutter in our lives is visible. That's because our minds and our hearts may be filled with personal regrets, damaged emotions, unhealthy relationships, and fear and uncertainty about the future.

Like me, you may dislike clutter but find that clearing it up and keeping it out can be difficult. When Donna and I bought a new home a few years ago, we moved all the stuff that wouldn't fit into our new home into the garage. Every spring we go through the ritual of spring cleaning. I take everything out of the garage and put it out on the driveway. Then Donna and I go through it and decide what we are going to throw away. Often I have decided to discard something, only to say, "I can't throw this away; I might need it at some point!" or "Maybe I'll take this to the office and store it there." I then move all the stuff back into the garage. Since we collect new things each year, I'm pulling out more items every spring.

Not only do we store all the stuff Donna and I have collected during thirty-eight years of marriage, but now that Andrea is on the mission field we have her stuff in there too. (And by the way, her dog has come to live with us.) With our son Derek going off to college, we'll be putting his extra stuff into the garage as well.

Clutter in our lives diverts us from our priorities.

Perhaps you've tried to jam too much into your life but have never classified it as clutter. For that reason, consider the three principles I have observed about this type of problem.

1. The more we go after in life, the more clutter we collect. Whether we go after more relationships, more money, more prestige, or more education—in whatever we pursue, we become like Velcro, don't we? Things begin to attach themselves to us, and we wind up with more sticking to us than we had before we started.
2. Clutter can be visible or invisible. It's often easier to deal with the visible clutter in our garages or our homes than the invisible clutter buried within us.
3. The way we deal with clutter will determine how well we do in life. I believe clutter has a way of slowing us down, keeping us from progressing and accomplishing the things God has for us to do.

The Bible tells us to live simple, peaceable lives. And yet even Christians continue to collect more, get more, and cling to more. Listen to the words of Jesus Christ to you: "Come to me, all you who are weary and burdened [and whose lives are full of clutter you have collected—my paraphrase], and I will give you rest. Take my yoke upon you and learn from me, for I am gentle and humble in heart, and you will find rest for your souls. For my yoke is easy and my burden is light" (Matthew 11:28-30). Just reading that verse is comforting to me. What a relief to know I can come to Christ, take the burdens off my back, and place them on him.

Since clutter is so annoying, why do we allow it into our lives? Understanding the seven reasons clutter may accumulate can help as you begin to think about the one small thing you could do to begin to free yourself from its control.

1. **You are overwhelmed.** Maybe you have a relationship that has really gone south; maybe you have a financial problem that seems insurmountable; maybe you have a cluttered desk or a cluttered schedule that you need to deal with. When you feel overwhelmed, you often get stuck. You are immobilized and don't know what to do next. You might feel so scattered that you are mentally paralyzed. When I was overwhelmed, I started hauling rocks. As you may recall, that led to some bad results!

2. **You don't know where to start.** You might ask yourself, *Where do I begin?* Whether it's a problem in a relationship, financial problems, or a messy house, the big question is the same: *What should I tackle first?*

3. **You have grown accustomed to the clutter.** I'm always amazed when I see a television report about someone like Doris. I ask myself, *How could that person stand to live like that?* But as a counselor, I know that people can grow accustomed to many things they really don't like or want to have around. The people whose homes are filled with garbage get used to it; that condition has become their normal way of life. I have worked with people whose lives were so mired in sin that it had become normal for them.

4. **You fear change.** We all love change if somebody else is changing, but we probably don't want to change ourselves. You (like me) may admit to having too many piles of stuff, but you know where things are in those piles, so you don't get rid of them.

5. **You need to control things, people, and outcomes.** Sometimes people hang on to things for unhealthy reasons. After you deal with the clutter of a broken relationship, you may miss the unhealthy thing you've been getting from that relationship. Perhaps you have been angry for so long in the relationship that without that anger, you would feel empty. If someone has wounded you deeply, you may hesitate to forgive that person because you don't want to give up the control you feel you have

over him or her. You may fear that doing so may make it easier for that person to hurt you again.

6. **You feel like you are competing.** The bumper sticker says it all: "The one with the most toys wins!" You may collect more and more stuff, thinking you need just one more item to keep up with your neighbors or friends. (Of course, there's always one more after that.)

7. **You let what is urgent get in the way of what is important.** Let's say as you're driving home from work one day you're focused on your plan to tackle your checkbook and bank statements right after dinner. You need to find out why the bank keeps charging you extra fees. But when you walk in the door, your wife calls to you from the laundry room, where she is mopping up water. The washing machine has malfunctioned, leaking all over the place. You quickly change your clothes and join her in the bucket brigade, stopping for a quick dinner. Afterward, you go back to the laundry room to try to uncover the source of the leak. The bank fees now seem far less urgent than the problem of the moment. Both need attention, but don't allow the urgent to cause you to forget about the important.

> *It's often easier to deal with the visible clutter in our garages or our homes than the invisible clutter buried within us.*

WHY CLUTTER?

Clutter can be a symptom of unresolved problems. When talking about managing emotions in chapter 7, I mentioned you can start at either end of the process. You can begin either by changing your actions or by altering your thinking, because both affect your emotions. Overcoming clutter is similar—you can start either by clearing out the obvious clutter or by solving the problem underlying your clutter.

Clearly, Doris had refused to address either. After pushing everyone in her life away, she tried to fill herself again by collecting and keeping every paper and knickknack. And she hoped that ordering just one more piece of jewelry or another figurine from a cable shopping show would fill the empty place inside her.

Scott Peck, author of *The Road Less Traveled*, said, "Problems do not go away. They must be worked through or else they remain, forever a barrier to the growth and development of the spirit."[6] Clutter is just a symptom of something else.

Clutter left unattended and problems left unresolved are two sides of the same coin. Both lead to mediocrity. If we could see our lives from God's perspective, many of us would be forced to admit that our lives are cluttered with all sorts of things that keep us from moving forward and receiving the abundant life he promises. We need to simplify our lives, eliminating the things that bog us down and keep us from doing what God says are priorities.

Successful people push back on events, interruptions, and people who threaten to crowd their lives with insignificant things. They throw away or recycle junk mail every day so it doesn't wind up in a collection like Doris's. They manage their relationships and their schedules so they have time for the people and causes most important to them.

ONE THING

Hang an erasable whiteboard wall calendar in your kitchen or another central location, noting each family member's appointments in a different color.

Other people are driven by the demands of others or by the incessant chatter of the media. They are easily interrupted and have difficulty saying no or prioritizing. Their homes and offices often become overladen with stacks and stacks of paper or other stuff that overwhelms them every time they walk in the door.

Let's look more closely at five kinds of clutter that can make our lives more difficult than they need to be: physical, mental, emotional, relational, and scheduling clutter. As you read, think about which of these five is your biggest challenge.

Physical clutter

Whether unread mail, your kids' toys, piles of laundry, or dirty dishes are strewn throughout your house, physical clutter is difficult to hide. Because it can lead you to waste valuable time hunting for items or keep you from inviting friends and neighbors into your home, this form of clutter can make you feel stressed, incompetent, and scattered.

Ironically, though, uncluttering your physical space may initially make you feel as if you have less, not more, control. I'm the type of person who, just as I'm ready to drop a piece of paper into the shredder, thinks, *Do I have a copy of this? What if my hard drive goes bad?* Yet as long as I let this type of anxiety prevent me from ordering and simplifying my life, I'm not really in control at all. Until you get a handle on physical clutter, you are likely to sacrifice peace of mind, a comfortable place to unwind, and the freedom to invite others into your home. Do one thing today to unclutter even one small part of your life—try starting with even one cluttered drawer.

Mental clutter

A cluttered mind has little room for a life-changing idea. And I don't believe that a cluttered mind can welcome and focus on God. That's a problem, because as Isaiah 26:3 (NKJV) says, "You will keep him in perfect peace, whose mind is stayed on You, because he trusts in You."

Have you ever wondered why, when you start your Bible reading or prayer time, a thousand thoughts rush into your mind—things you need to do, issues you need to resolve, items you can't forget, people you need to call? That is mental clutter.

Here are some other symptoms of mental clutter:

You feel frustrated by your undisciplined thoughts. Proverbs 16:3 (NKJV) says, "Commit your works to the LORD, and your thoughts will be established." But instead of following his ways, we often dwell on our immediate feelings, experiences, and thoughts. You may rationalize an impulsive purchase at the mall by thinking, *I need it . . . I deserve it . . . I'm going to get it.* Later on, knowing that you really couldn't afford it, you feel regret. The same thing can happen when it comes to eating. Yes, your doctor told you to cut way back on the sugar, but everyone else is ordering dessert, so why shouldn't you get a piece of your favorite chocolate chip cheesecake? Undisciplined thoughts are clutter that distract and tempt us, often sabotaging our goals.

You accept untested assumptions. An untested assumption is anything you believe without verifying it. Assumptions can lead to wrong conclusions that get you into trouble. General Custer assumed his soldiers couldn't be defeated, and they were slaughtered. Bernard Madoff might have assumed he wouldn't get caught committing securities fraud and go to jail, but he did. As a nation we believed we could use credit with abandon, and we've learned a hard lesson. Many in the United States assume that God is not going to bring judgment on us for our national and individual sins of abortion, greed, addiction, slander, and more. That is a wrong assumption.

> ## ONE THING
>
> Keep an "external hard drive" for your mind—such as a BlackBerry or notebook and pen—close by your bed, on your desk, or in your car to capture distracting but important thoughts. Whenever your sleep, quiet time, or another focused activity is interrupted by a great idea or a nagging concern, record it right away so you can concentrate again on your task at hand (or fall back to sleep more easily).

Do you assume that you can keep spending because your salary increases will outpace your debts? Or that you can continue to abuse your health by overeating, not exercising, or consuming drugs or alcohol with no negative health effects? Or that your opposite-sex friendship will remain just that—an innocent friendship? The assumption that it will never happen to me or us or our country is a mistake. As 1 Thessalonians 5:21 (NKJV) advises, "Test all things; hold fast what is good." We must test and verify our assumptions.

You wrestle with recurring unclean thoughts. This kind of mental clutter is prompted by dozens of images we see every day in the media and all around us. It, too, can have serious consequences, such as an addiction to pornography.

Identify one piece of mental clutter in your life today and eliminate it.

Emotional clutter

Your heart can be the dumping ground for every emotion you don't know how to handle—creating emotional clutter that leaves no room in your heart to genuinely love and care for others. As a counselor, I have discovered that many people don't know what to do with anger, frustration, or loneliness. When these feelings are not handled properly, they stay in our hearts, which become more and more cluttered and nonfunctioning.

Here are some symptoms of emotional clutter:

- You react instead of respond in certain situations. Unhealthy emotions may be so close to the surface that you react in a way you don't want to. Do you yell at your kids or your spouse? Are you critical or explosive toward your coworkers? Reacting instead of responding can be a sign of emotional overload or clutter.

- You can't identify your feelings. In chapter 7 we talked about the need to understand your emotions and how you feel at any given time. If you have emotional clutter, you may be shutting down your feelings because they are too overwhelming. What are you feeling right now?

- You feel trapped by your feelings. Anger traps people. I get calls every day on my radio program from people who say, "I'm struggling with anger; help me deal with my irritation." Have others expressed concern about your emotions? Have you resolved time and again that you will answer calmly when someone says something that triggers your anger, but each time the situation arises, you blow it? Feeling trapped by your emotions is a symptom of emotional clutter.

- You feel unable to forgive a hurt or wrong done to you. Unforgiveness and the resulting bitterness and hatred create severe problems. Forgiving is difficult, it is painful, and it requires that you give up something you want to hold on to, but God says we must do it. First John 3:14-15 (NKJV) says, "We know that we have passed from death to life, because we love the brethren. He who does not love his brother abides in death.

Whoever hates his brother is a murderer, and you know that no murderer has eternal life abiding in him."

Did you know that when you hate someone for a wrong he or she has done to you, you really hurt yourself and not the other person? Forgiving that person will actually benefit you because unforgiveness will only eat you up inside, ruining your life and even your health. You don't have to wait until you "feel" like forgiving someone. It's okay to tell God that you don't feel forgiving but that you are willing to forgive in obedience to what he has said. It will then be up to him to make your feelings catch up with your obedient act of forgiving.

ONE THING

Talking with a counselor about your inability to forgive someone who deeply wounded you may be one of the most courageous and freeing things you'll ever do.

You are aware that your attitude is unhealthy. We have talked about changing our attitudes in chapter 6, but here I want to help you identify emotional clutter. If you know your attitude is poor but you seem unable to permanently change it, go back to the action steps in that chapter and do one thing each day to improve your attitude. Remember that your attitude is within your control.

Today identify one area of emotional clutter in your life and get rid of it.

Relationship clutter

Clutter in relationships develops when small or large conflicts that exist between two or more people are either denied or not resolved. They then become ever-present irritants in the relationship.

Cluttered relationships create fatigue and frustration. You might feel the nagging presence of unresolved issues that never seem to end or be resolved. A number of years ago I found a poem called "Walls" by an unknown author that was included in *Unlocking the Secrets of Your Childhood Memories*, which I wrote with Kevin Leman. I used it again in my book *Starved for Affection*. This excerpt is pertinent to our discussion on relationship clutter as well, since it so vividly portrays how distance grows between two people.

> Slowly, the wall between them rose, cemented by the mortar of
>   indifference.
> One day, reaching out to touch each other, they found a barrier
> they could not penetrate, and recoiling from the coldness of the stone,
> each retreated from the stranger on the other side.
> For when love dies it is not in a moment of angry battle, nor when fiery
>   bodies lose their heat. It lies panting, exhausted, expiring at the
>   bottom of a wall it could not scale.

Just as Doris's stuff accumulated in her home layer by layer, making it so crowded that the police could hardly walk through her living room, so the frustration between two people can grow layer by layer and clutter their relationship.

Emotional clutter and relationship clutter do overlap. But while emotional clutter exists internally, relationship clutter involves another person or persons. Here are three steps for resolving relationship clutter:

1. **Identify the problem.** I suggest you begin by writing down what you see as the nagging issue when you think about your relationships. Start with one relationship and figure out the problem. Often on the radio I challenge callers by asking, "Is that really the problem you are facing?" Often the true problem is something else entirely.

2. **Identify how you contribute to the problem.** It takes a humble spirit to admit, "You know, I was a real jerk!" Can you do that? Earlier I mentioned how I had to go to someone and ask for forgiveness after I had been difficult. I had a long litany of things the other person had done against me, but I also had that list of "jerk-like" things I had done. It was easier for me to focus on what the other person had done wrong. Acknowledging my wrongdoing took introspection, awareness, and humility.

3. **Reconcile if you can.** Not every relationship is reconcilable. But

when possible it's best to take the high road and be the one willing to reconcile and restore a relationship, letting go of the hurt.

Schedule clutter

If you allow other people to control your schedule, you may not have time to fit in more important opportunities. The following symptoms indicate whether you experience schedule clutter:

1. Do you feel like the many interruptions and demands of other people and things control your schedule, preventing you from accomplishing what you know you need to do?
2. Do you focus on the important things in your schedule, or do you roam from activity to activity without completing any of them?

Information overload from the Internet, TV, cell phones, and other technologies can leave you feeling buried. Likewise, you may take on more and more projects at work, afraid that if you don't you may be overlooked for that promotion or, worse, lose your job in the next round of layoffs. You may succumb to the guilt that people at your kids' school or sports team put on you to do more, give more, and sell more magazines or candy bars. And as we mentioned in chapter 9, today's world offers plenty of opportunities to waste time.

Learning to say no, both to other people and to the part of you that just wants to coast, is essential if you're ever going to bring your schedule back under control. You can also refuse to let less important things distract you from those activities that really matter.

One thing you can do for yourself today is to take control of your own schedule to the extent you can.

CLEARING THE CLUTTER

Albert Einstein said, "It's not that I'm so smart, it's just that I stay with problems longer." Isn't that true? If we were committed to addressing the problems in our lives—like physical clutter, mental clutter, emotional clutter, relationship clutter, or schedule clutter—we would find victory.

When I was a teenager, Virgil Brock became a friend of our family.

Virgil was a contemporary of the famous evangelist Billy Sunday, and he wrote some of the best-known worship songs of the early twentieth century, including "Beyond the Sunset." When we met him, Virgil was an old man with a lot of wisdom who had been very successful at a lot of things. He nearly dripped with wisdom.

By the end of his life, Virgil had intentionally uncluttered his life. He didn't want to leave behind a mess like Doris's for others to clean up. He gave away everything he had to Christian causes. He had no regrets or unfinished business, and he didn't

> **ONE THING**
>
> Decide as a family how many extracurricular activities each child may sign up for. Then stick to that number.

hang on to a lot of stuff. In fact, he lived the last couple of years of his life in a mobile home on the grounds of Youth Haven Ranch in Michigan.

One snowy Sunday morning in February, Virgil left his mobile home to go to church. Before he got across the camp, he collapsed and died with a Bible literally on his chest. My brother, Larry, found him.

Larry said that when those close to him went through Virgil's belongings, they found very little. Besides the clothes he had on his back, he had given almost everything away. He showed me how to live and how to die. Live for God and die free.

My desire is that when I die, I am free—with no regrets and no mental, emotional, or relationship clutter. I don't want to go to my grave with unresolved issues with people. So I need to clean up my clutter now while I still can—just like Virgil did.

ONE SMALL THING TO BEGIN CHANGING YOUR LIFE

- Identify one area of clutter that you want to tackle. Physical clutter may be a good place to start. Set one goal that's achievable—don't say you're going to clean out your attic, basement, and garage and have them all spick-and-span this week. Instead, choose a bite-size project. That may mean pulling out and cleaning one drawer in your messiest room. Even if the whole room is a disaster, you will have taken control and can say, "This drawer is clean." It will give you the momentum to tackle another drawer the following day.

- Choose something you can wrestle to the ground. You may recognize, for instance, that scattered thinking is keeping you from acting on what you know you need to do. Or perhaps you're stuck with relationship clutter and have been avoiding holding a much-needed discussion with a loved one. Either way, commit to resolving the issue. That may mean setting a date on your calendar or finding someone to hold you accountable.

- Find someone who will hold you accountable, someone who can call you and say, "How are you doing with that relationship clutter you told me you were going to take care of this week? How can I pray with you?" Often it helps if you are mutually accountable— you and the other person are each working on something and being held accountable by the other.

- Block your calendar for fifteen-minute increments when you work on your clutter. Once you complete the first area, use those fifteen minutes to tackle the next area. Before you know it, your life will feel a lot cleaner.

12
THE POWER OF ONE THING TO CHANGE THE QUESTIONS YOU ASK

*The uncreative mind can spot wrong answers, but it takes
a very creative mind to spot wrong questions.*
—SIR ANTONY RUPERT JAY, BRITISH AUTHOR

Rolando is an expert at asking questions. A foreign correspondent, he has been all over the world, covering wars in the Middle East, coups in Africa, and natural disasters in Indonesia. He is well trained in the "five *W*s and an *H*" that reporters everywhere use to develop their stories and provide the who, what, when, where, why, and how behind a news event.

Yet after several grueling assignments, Rolando discovered it was becoming more difficult to interview people who had just suffered a major tragedy. Questioning the grieving mother about what had happened to her dead son or asking the bleeding soldier how the ambush had occurred was critical if he was to do his job. But it was difficult for him emotionally, even after a decade of seeing up close nearly every human tragedy he could imagine.

Despite the emotional toll, Rolando loved his work. When he was offered a promotion that would allow him to return to the States and cover politics in the nation's capital, he turned it down in favor of his worldwide travels. Yet that forced Rolando, an introspective person, to ask himself a tough question: why did he keep going to war-torn areas, far from his family and home, even when he had the opportunity to come back to the States for good?

Why, Lord? I feel like you want me to continue to cover these tragedies, even though they break my heart and keep me awake at night, he prayed. *Why do I feel compelled to stay in the field even though it's so difficult?*

Rolando was asking one of the most important questions that exists—*why*. Why do we do what we do? I believe that if more of us asked ourselves the tough questions, like the motives behind our actions, we would have more successful lives and relationships.

You may be surprised that I include the inability to ask good questions on my list of the nine things that trigger most of the difficulties I encounter in my work as a counselor. Few of us are taught that formulating questions is a vital life skill. Yet consider the power that some questions have. How do you feel when asking (or being asked) one of these questions:

- Is it benign?
- How did this happen?
- What were you thinking?
- Did my child come through surgery all right?
- Did you get the job?
- Will you marry me?

Good questions are direct and elicit critical information. That's why our success will be determined, in part, by the kind of questions we ask—of ourselves and of others.

Ben Franklin said that time is the "stuff of life." I would add: I think questions are the stuff of life—they are the key to knowing others, learning, solving problems, discovering, and understanding ourselves. Have you ever noticed the root of the word *question*? It's *quest*, a search or pursuit to find or obtain something.

Successful people are not afraid to ask themselves tough questions and then go deep to get the answers. Unsuccessful people avoid the tough questions, and if they come across one, either they won't answer it or they avoid it. Of course, it's not enough to pose good questions, which is why successful people are also good listeners. Most people tend to be so busy formulating their next statement that they hear very little of what is said to them.

Notice that success is dependent, not just on asking questions, but on asking the *right* questions. John Sawatsky, a Canadian journalist, teacher, and interviewing coach for ESPN, describes the skill as something between an art and a science. "Questions," he says, "are precise instruments—ask the wrong question, and even a cooperative interview subject may not be able to give you the information you need."[7]

Asking questions of yourself and others is important. Even more critical is asking *good* questions. Let's talk about how you can do one thing to ask better questions of yourself and others.

FROM THE MOUTHS OF BABES

When we are little, we ask zillions of questions. If you are a parent, you undoubtedly remember the way your children asked, "Why?" about everything, or so it seemed. "Why do I have to do that?" "Why does that happen?" "Why did he do that?" "What does that mean?" Sadly, that propensity is quickly discouraged. The message too many children get from their parents and some teachers is, "Stop asking so many questions, and just do what I tell you to do." By retirement age, most people ask just a few questions a day.

Having said that, toward the end of our lives, we are able to ask better and more reflective questions about how we have lived and what really matters. We can learn a lot from the reflections of people who, approaching the end of life, have learned valuable lessons by looking back.

Yet between childhood and old age, we become experts at answering questions instead of asking questions. After all, we are evaluated on

ONE THING

Value your children's questions, using them to affirm your children and get to know them better:

- Don't brush off the silly-sounding questions of the young children in your life.
- Don't cut off challenging questions from teens.

how well we answer questions on tests, in job interviews, and in the workplace. We are rewarded, or at least promoted to the next grade level, for answering questions correctly.

But we aren't taught to ask better questions. In school, we don't get a grade based on the questions we ask, except, perhaps, for a little check mark at the bottom of the report card where our teacher evaluates our participation. What matters most, though, is the grades at the top of the report. I've never heard a teacher say, "You couldn't answer the test questions, but you asked some great questions, so I'm going to give you an A."

Though we are trained to answer questions, the questions we *ask* will determine our future. Your life today is the result of your answer to a question such as:

- Is God real?
- Is God going to provide for me?
- Can I trust people?
- Am I capable of doing that?

The types of questions you ask have made you the way you are today.

QUESTIONS IN THE BIBLE

We tend to think of the Bible in terms of instructions and principles about our relationship with Christ. But Scripture includes 6,695 uses of the words *what*, *why*, *how*, *when*, and *where*. Many of these are challenges in the form of questions. Some of these queries are rhetorical and require no answer. Others demand that we address key issues in our lives.

As followers of God, then, we need to seek God's direction continuously, asking, "God, what do you have for me in this situation? What is the right thing to do?" While that may seem obvious, we often just go ahead and do something or make a decision without asking God for his wisdom.

Acts 16 records a Philippian jailer asking the most important question of all after living through the greatest fright of his life. When a powerful earthquake shook his jail, the doors opened and the chains of Paul and Silas, along with the other prisoners', were loosened, allowing them to leave. The jailer was about to kill himself for failing in his responsibility to keep the prisoners under guard when Paul said, "Don't harm yourself! We are all here!" (Acts 16:28).

The jailer saw that they were free but had decided not to leave. He then asked a profound and life changing question, "Sirs, what must I do to be saved?" (Acts 16:30).

I wonder what I would have asked if I were the jailer. More than likely, my question would have been something like, "How did you do that?" "When are they going to come and take these guys away for their trial so I don't have to be under this constant stress?" or "How do I get them back in their chains so I don't lose my head?" If the Philippian jailer had asked those questions, he might have gotten answers, but he would have missed the most profound answer of all: "Believe in the Lord Jesus, and you will be saved!" (Acts 16:31).

NOT ALL QUESTIONS ARE EQUAL

As the account of the Philippian jailer proves, it's not enough to ask questions. We must be intentional about asking the right ones. Suppose a single twentysomething was swept off his or her feet by a romantic partner. Within a few weeks, the pair are convinced they are soul mates, and they begin window-shopping at jewelry stores. What if the first question the couple asks is, "When should we get married?"

A better question for each person to ask is, "Is getting married to this person God's best for me?" That question should be asked (and answered) long before they talk about setting a wedding date.

Many people start looking for another job because they wonder, *Could I earn more money?* or *I wonder if I could find a job that's closer to home and cut down on my commute.* A better question is, *Lord, what do you want for my life? Does my current job fit your plans for me?*

What about this question: "Can I afford to go to college?" Most people would have to say no. In fact, this response has kept many people from continuing their educations. A better question would be, "What education or training should I pursue to follow God's plans for my life?" That question puts you on an entirely different course from the question of affordability.

A question I am often asked on our radio program is, "What did I do wrong that led my child to reject Christ?" These parents are guilt ridden, focused on the things they didn't do but wish they had. A better question for a parent with a rebellious child would be, "How can I best respond to my son's spiritual rebellion against God?"

How about this one: "How can I get my kids to listen to me?" A better question is, "What am I doing—or not doing—now that makes my kids disobey me in the first place?" Or this one: "When should I retire?" when maybe a better question is, "Does God want me to retire?" Or "Why is my spouse so angry all the time?" A better question is, "How should I respond when my spouse gets so angry?"

> ## ONE THING
>
> **When facing a tough decision, don't just ask yourself, *Should I or shouldn't I?* Seek to get at the deeper questions that will help you discern God's best for your life.**

Picasso said that computers are useless because they can only give you answers. Isn't that true. It takes human beings with the minds God gave us to ask the really important questions of life. Mundane questions produce a mundane life. When you start to ask better questions, you will find better answers to live a more passion-filled, focused, and intentional life.

Here are some examples of better questions to ask yourself:

- How do I keep defeating myself?
- Am I really a follower of Christ, or am I just going through the motions?
- What is the true meaning of my relationship with Jesus Christ?
- How did I end up where I am today?
- What can I do to get where I know God wants me to go?
- What does my family need from me that I am not giving them now?
- What would happen to my family if I died today?
- How do others know that God is real in my life?
- How are my friendships benefiting my life?
- Where does God want me to be in five years?
- What is my greatest strength, and am I exercising it in my life?
- How does God view me?

- How do I view myself?
- How do others view me?
- What would happen if I decided to go back to school?
- Should my spouse and I adopt a child?
- Why am I so difficult to get along with?
- How am I making things better for my coworkers?
- Where am I most needed?

These questions will make you think. They will lead you to productive and satisfying answers. Learning to ask better questions is like learning a foreign language—it's hard at first, but it becomes easier the more you practice. The results are well worth it.

Some people never master this skill because the only questions they ever ask are, "What am I going to wear?" "How am I going to get to work?" "Where am I going for lunch?" "What am I going to watch on television tonight?" "Where will I go on vacation?" "How am I going to spend my money?" Obviously we need to make these decisions; however, they don't have a lot of meaning. While such questions are nonthreatening because they don't force people to examine themselves closely enough to feel uncomfortable, they also don't lead to significant growth.

Asking important questions can change your life. Every day we evaluate things and situations and make choices. The better the quality of our questions, the better the quality of the answers will be. It's not that we need to ask ourselves profound, earthshaking questions all day long. The quality of our questions is more important than the quantity.

NOT JUST FOR JOURNALISTS

Chances are your high school English teacher taught you the six questions that every reporter needs to know. But while you may not have given them much thought since your final exam, these words are tools you can use to ask better questions of yourself and others. The answers to *who, when,* or *where* are generally fairly obvious, so they're less likely to elicit deep information. But the others can be especially useful whether you're asking questions of yourself or others.

What?

What questions are based on action. "What happened?" "What should I do next?" "What do you need?" They demand an answer and require action. The young ruler in Luke 18 came to Christ and asked, in essence, "What do I need to do to follow you? I've done everything right, I've followed all the laws, I've given my money. What must I do to inherit eternal life?" It's a great question, very similar to that of the Philippian jailer. Jesus perceived that the one thing the young ruler needed to do was to sell all he had and follow him. The young man had asked a great question and gotten a great answer, but he wasn't willing to do it. Are you willing to obey a great answer when you get one?

Here are some instances where *what* questions work well:

- When you're unclear as to what is going on around you, you need to ask, "Hey, what's going on here?" Many of us make decisions without having a clear understanding of the situation, and *what* questions can help.
- When you need to make a decision. *What* questions drive us to make a decision. What do I need to do? What needs to happen now? What am I responsible for in this situation?

Why?

Why questions are useful for getting clarification. They are good for introspection, and they help us understand the root of an issue. "Why is my family falling apart in front of me?" "Why is my health deteriorating?" *Why* questions force us to look inside, not at other people.

In Luke 6:41-42, Jesus asks, "Why do you look at the speck of sawdust in your brother's eye and pay no attention to the plank in your own eye? How can you say to your brother, 'Brother, let me take the speck out of your eye,' when you yourself fail to see the plank in your own eye?" The question is, "Why do I do that?" It forces you to go deeper in understanding your own motives in your relationships with other people.

In contemporary Western culture, we tend to focus on what to do and how to get it done. "What do I need to do to get my kids to start listening to me?" "What do I have to do to make my husband less angry?" We want to *do* something before asking the more significant question of why our kids aren't listening or what is causing our spouse's anger in the first place.

The *why* questions are often very difficult ones. "Why does God allow suffering?" "Why did my marriage fail?" "Why is life so unfair?" The danger is that *why* questions can get us stuck so that we never get to the *what, when,* and *how* questions that could help us take action.

Some *why* questions can't be answered. "Why me, Lord?"

ONE THING

When tempted to ask God why something happened, focus instead on

- *what*—what does God want you to learn from it; and
- *how*—how can God use this in your life to glorify himself and comfort others?

"Why did this have to happen to my kid?" We can get so wrapped up in the *why* questions that we never simply say, "God, it is in your hands; I trust you completely" and start moving forward by faith. We need to start asking God, "What do I need to do now, and how do I do it?"

Situations that call for *why* questions:

- when you are unclear about your purpose
- when you are confused
- when understanding motive is important

How?

In Romans 10:14-15 (NKJV) we read, "How then shall they call on Him in whom they have not believed? And how shall they believe in Him of whom they have not heard? And how shall they hear without a preacher? And how shall they preach unless they are sent?" These are rhetorical questions whose obvious answer is, "We need to go out and share the gospel. That is how it is going to be done."

How questions are what I call "process questions," which ask for the steps to make something happen, the process needed to get it done. Once you have the answer to how, you can move ahead and get the necessary help to do a job well.

How questions provide the process, but they can also be revealing. Ask yourself, *How can I do this in a way that honors God? How can I be a better spouse or employee or parent?*

Some good uses for *how* questions are:

- when you want to learn something new
- when you want to do a better job than you are doing now
- when you need help

QUESTIONS FOR OTHERS

Asking ourselves good questions is important. But the questions we ask others are also very important. Again, we can develop our skill at asking penetrating questions and really listening to the answers.

Questions can either elicit an answer or shut down conversation. They can make someone mad or begin the healing process. They can help clarify issues or muddy the waters.

You've undoubtedly known people who are able to draw others out in conversation. Perhaps someone at your church welcomes new people and seems to know all about them by the end of their first visit. Such people have perfected the art of the question and also the skill of listening. Just peppering strangers with questions won't get you very far, but displaying a genuine openness and interest in them is likely to open doors to conversation and friendship.

I heard leadership expert John Maxwell say on one of his monthly mentoring CDs that he spends more time preparing his questions before meeting with someone than he actually spends in the meeting with the person. That's because he wants to learn and get the best information. He said, "If I have an hour with somebody who knows more than I know and if I ask them silly questions, I'm going to get silly answers. I want deep questions that are going to draw out the kind of answers that are going to be important for my life."

Author John Brady, in *The Craft of Interviewing*, said, "For every minute spent in an interview, at least ten minutes should be spent in preparation."[8] That means that a one-hour interview would require ten hours of preparation. Questions are serious business!

So spend time thinking about your questions. What's the best way to ask your kids questions? your spouse? your coworkers?

The open-ended question

An open-ended question, asked in the right way and at the right time, can be very effective. Open-ended questions are those that leave room for a fuller response; closed-ended questions are those that require a simple one- or two-word answer, such as yes or no.

Which questions below do you feel more like answering?

1. What are your views on . . . ?
2. What is the significance of . . . ?
3. Did you do what I asked you to do today?
4. Did you learn anything new at school today?
5. Who broke the vase in the living room?
6. How did you feel when . . . ?

The open-ended questions are numbers 1, 2, and 6. Such how, why, and what questions encourage another person to describe, explain, and amplify. Closed-ended questions like numbers 3, 4, and 5 elicit brief, unequivocal responses.

Sometimes a good open-ended question will not yield an immediate answer. It will, however, get the other person thinking. Be patient. Grilling him or her with endless follow-up questions usually produces little except frustration for both of you.

The tough questions

I once was scheduled to appear on *The 700 Club* on the same day as Josh McDowell. I had never met Josh before, but after he introduced himself, Josh looked me right in the eye and said, "Have you been faithful to your wife?" He skipped "Hi, how are you?" and went straight to the heart.

Fortunately, I could honestly say, "Yes, I am and have been." But what a challenge. If I were to walk up to you and ask you if you have been faithful to your spouse, how would you answer?

I'm not suggesting you regularly go up to strangers and ask them personal questions. However, the willingness of a fellow believer to ask you the tough questions can be a great blessing. After all, Hebrews 10:24 says believers are to "spur one another on toward love and good deeds." Allow people you trust to ask you tough questions instead of only questions like, "Who won the basketball game last night?" or "How's the weather?" or "How are things going at work?"

ONE THING

Before having a tough talk with a friend or loved one, or before you head to an important work meeting, take a few minutes to write out open-ended questions that will elicit helpful information.

Remember Rolando? He was not afraid to ask himself the tough questions as he struggled in his career. He asked God again and again, *Am I on the right path, Lord? I sense you want me to continue to report on these tragedies. Am I hearing you correctly?*

After wrestling with these questions for months, Rolando finally felt he got an answer. While he didn't hear an audible voice, he had the strong impression of the words, *What you do for the least of these, you do for me.* Rolando understood that his job enabled him to give a voice to the victims of tragedies the world over, and in doing so, he was right where God wanted him to be.

ONE SMALL THING TO BEGIN CHANGING YOUR LIFE

- If you are not used to asking yourself the hard questions, read the list on pages 136–137. Select the one that intrigues you most and take some time to journal your response. The power of asking the one right question at the right time to the right person could change your life. Remember that sometimes the most important questions are those you ask yourself about you.

- What is one question you think about often—something you worry about or regret or ponder frequently without reaching an answer? (Examples: Why can't my boss see that I deserve a promotion? Why did I invest in that stock last year? Why do I always say the wrong thing when I try to talk to my teenage daughter?) Now revise your question to make it a better, more productive, positive question. (Examples: How can I help my boss see my contributions more clearly? What will be a good investment strategy for me for the upcoming twelve months? What encouraging words can I say to my daughter when I drive her to school tomorrow morning?)

- Check your motivation in an important area of your life by asking *why*. (Examples: Why do I spend all those hours at the office? Why did I quit teaching Sunday school last year?) Ask God to help you understand your motivation.

- Jot down three difficult questions and ask them often to keep yourself honest. (Examples include: What does my family need from me that I am not giving them now? How do others know that God is real in my life? Where does God want me to be in five years? What is my greatest strength, and am I exercising it in my life?)

- Write down three open-ended questions you could ask a friend or family member. (Examples include: How did you feel when . . . ? What do you think about . . . ? Could you tell me more about . . . ?)

- Ask these open-ended questions of a family member or friend, and write down his or her responses to consider what insights that person provides.

13
The Power of One Thing to Change How You Make Decisions

There is no more miserable human being than one in whom nothing is habitual but indecision.

—William James, nineteenth-century American psychologist

Making a decision and then acting on that decision can change your life. It has for me in my ministry work, and it can for you in your family or business life too. As CEO of Family Life Communications, I realized a few years ago that we needed to make an important decision concerning our ministry's future direction. After forty years of building up our radio network of stations, it was tempting just to coast along and let things happen. We had built a network of thirty-seven stations around the country and developed our worldwide *Intentional Living* broadcast ministry; we had been successful in meeting the needs of a lot of people. Everything was in order; everything was being done; we were moving forward. In my heart, though, I felt we were becoming somewhat complacent. I knew there must be more—a way to reach more people. It was a healthy and needed discontent.

God had given to us a great tool in radio, and I knew it was time to make a decision. We needed to fish or cut bait when it came to growth and outreach. It would have been easier to lay back and keep doing what we'd always been doing, but I knew God expected more and that we could do more. I asked myself, *Are we going to move forward, or are we going to allow ourselves to stay stuck where we are today?* Were we willing to stretch, to risk, to grow in order to reach more people for Christ? Or would the ministry just drift along? It came down to one decision—to risk and grow or to keep doing the same thing.

I prayed and talked to our board, to Donna, and to our ministry leadership about where we needed to go and the need to make that one decision. After a time of prayer and planning, I made that one decision—to trust God, step out, risk—to grow. I told my team that the decision had been made and now it was time to act. We were going to pray together, plan together, and risk together so we could take our ministry to an entirely new level of outreach, effectiveness, and impact.

That one decision made at one moment in time on one day in time, followed up with lots of "one thing" actions, resulted in the following positive outcomes over the next three years:

1. We added seven new stations to our owned and operated radio network.
2. We doubled the number of people we reach each day by radio.
3. We substantially reduced the cost of reaching each person.
4. We improved the quality of our on-air sound.
5. We developed an Internet radio station—www.myflr.org.
6. We developed a twenty-four-hour prayer ministry. On one day in early 2009 over four thousand people called in for prayer.
7. We created thousands of new Intentional Living resources for people.

All of this came from one decision acted upon over an extended period of time—it all resulted from the power of one decision.

Deciding to grow our radio ministry was scary for me, and at times I felt very much alone. The funny thing about decision making is that it all seems clearer to you the further you get beyond the decision. At the time it wasn't all that clear how it would work out, but looking back now it's apparent that I made the right decision. As Lady Bird Johnson advised, "Become so wrapped up in something that you forget to be afraid."

Because of this experience, I understand how hard it can be to make decisions and actually begin to implement change. I once taught a lesson called "Ready, Aim, Fire!" about the importance of finally acting on our decisions. Many people get ready and aim ... but they never pull the trigger. Without that last step and bold action, however, we will never advance.

What one decision do you need to make now that would change your life for the better in the future? Have you been asking yourself:

Should I go back to school?
Should we move closer to family?
Should I marry this person?
Should we have more children?
Should I apply for that job?

Intentional living is all about deciding how you live rather than allowing life just to happen. In the Old Testament, Joshua chose to make God the center of his family, and it changed everything for him (see Joshua 24). As a young king, Solomon chose to ask God for wisdom instead of riches, and God granted him great wisdom along with worldly wealth and fame (see 2 Chronicles 1).

Even before your feet hit the floor each morning, you begin making choices and decisions. Some are important; others are not. Should you get up today or hit the snooze button one more time? Will you get to work on time or be late? Will you honor your marriage or play the edge? Will you spend time planning for the future or simply veg out in front of the television?

ONE THING

Get in the habit of asking God, within just a few minutes of waking up, to direct your decisions that day. Then listen for his response, whether in his Word, in the wisdom of others, or in your circumstances.

Choose today how you will live before life chooses for you. In the last chapter, we talked about the wisdom of asking yourself good questions that will provide fresh insights. Answering the following questions can give you some helpful insights into the way you make decisions:

- What choices have you put off for too long?
- What decisions do you need to make right now based on the prayers, plans, and preparation you've already completed?
- Have you made any choices that you now regret? By thinking through the factors that led to one or more decisions with a negative outcome, you may uncover a pattern of thinking or action that you'll want to avoid in the future. For instance, if you regret dropping out of college, quitting a demanding job, or leaving your old church, you may begin to see your tendency to quit when a position becomes too challenging.

FREEDOM WITH RESPONSIBILITY

God gives us the freedom to make many choices about how we live. However, that doesn't mean that decision making is always easy. God's Word is full of stories of men and women who had to make difficult choices. Abraham had to choose whether to obey God when he told him to sacrifice his beloved son, Isaac. Queen Esther had to choose whether to risk her life to go before the king to try to save her people.

But what if Abraham or Esther had simply said, "I'm going to think and pray some more about what God wants me to do"? Often when we as Christians need to make a decision or solve a problem, we say, "I'm going to pray about it" or "I'm going to trust God about that." These are good things to do, but sometimes we don't get around to making a decision. We don't act.

Every day on our program I talk to people who are not making decisions, or they are making the wrong decisions that are destroying their finances, their health, or their relationships. Fortunately, Scripture outlines a process to help us become prayerful, deliberate decision makers. When we make good decisions in a God-honoring way, our lives and the lives of those around us will improve.

One of my models for biblical decision making is Nehemiah, a Jew who lived about four hundred years before Christ. As the cupbearer and a confidant to the Persian king, Nehemiah was greatly saddened when he heard about the poor condition of Jerusalem following his people's exile from Judea. He had a difficult decision to make: would he try to leverage his favored status with the king into an opportunity to go to Jerusalem and lead the people there in rebuilding the city's walls? As distraught as he was by Jerusalem's decline, Nehemiah knew that such a request could raise the ire of the king, who had made it clear once before that he didn't want Jerusalem rebuilt (see Ezra 4:21-22). Would Nehemiah risk his personal comfort and status—maybe even his life—to seek permission to travel to Jerusalem?

As we consider what Nehemiah did, we find valuable insights into how to make decisions with confidence.

Pray first

Challenged by the need of his country, Nehemiah spent much time in prayer, fasting, and mourning before doing anything else. Nehemiah 1:5-11 includes a heartfelt prayer asking for God's mercy and direction.

It's not until the next spring that we see him beginning to make decisions and act on them. (You can read about it in Nehemiah 2.) Though terrified, Nehemiah humbly asked the king's permission to go to Jerusalem. Not only did King Artaxerxes give Nehemiah permission to go to Jerusalem, he provided letters of protection as well as the timber the Jews would need to rebuild the city walls. In the following chapters, we see how the lives of God's people were changed and the walls of Jerusalem were rebuilt because this man made a decision after he got off of his knees in prayer.

Let's contrast Nehemiah with Jonah. When God commanded this prophet to go to Nineveh and warn the people there to repent, Jonah rejected God's instructions, got on a ship, and ended up in the belly of a giant fish. He made a decision, but it was the wrong one. He didn't consider the consequences of his decision, and it cost him big time.

Note that Nehemiah prayed in chapter 1 before he acted. On the other hand, Jonah acted first (in a way contrary to God's will); in fact, he prayed only when he was inside the fish, which we read about in Jonah chapter 2. I think many of us Christians are Jonah chapter 2 pray-ers! We decide to pray only after we are in the belly of the fish—when we're in trouble. When we make decisions, we need to be sure we are on our knees in prayer in chapter 1—*before* we act in chapter 2.

It doesn't need to be a fancy prayer; just pour out your heart to the Lord. "God, help me! I don't know what I am going to do. I don't know what you want me to do. I need the power of the Holy Spirit to make this decision. You are not writing your direction on my wall, and I've got to make a decision. I've got this teenage son or daughter who is driving me crazy and, God, I've got to do something."

ONE THING

If you're trying to make a major decision, consider using a journal to sort out your thoughts, hopes, apprehensions, and impressions, along with any factual information that might help you decide.

Pray before you make a decision about that teenager, your marriage, or your job. And when you pray, remember that it is a two-way street. Just as you ask God to listen to you, so must you wait to hear him speak to you. The apostle James offers a wonderful promise to believers: "If you need wisdom, ask our generous God, and he will give it to you. He will not rebuke you for asking" (James 1:5, NLT). As you pray, read Scripture, seek the counsel of mature believers, and see how circumstances are coming together, you may better understand the Lord's will for your situation.

Don't forget to act

As important as prayer is, it must never be used as an excuse not to act. Once the Lord has clearly shown you what one thing you need to do next, be ready to move forward. The following simple, yet effective, process will help you act deliberately but not recklessly:

1. **Make the decision or goal clear.** As I've worked with people over many years, I have observed that most of us are not very clear on what the real issue is. A woman called the program and said, "I'm trying to decide how I can communicate better with my husband. He is difficult; he's angry. For twenty years I've had to deal with him being up and down, and I don't know what to do about it. I want to be able to break through this facade so we can talk about the real, core issues in his life. Can you help me?"

I started to dig a little deeper and found out that her husband was an alcoholic. She then explained that he had also been diagnosed with bipolar disorder. As I continued asking questions, I learned she had evidence that he was not being faithful to her. It became clear, as we went a little deeper, that this guy really had no interest in getting help for his alcoholism, he was inconsistent on the treatment for his bipolar disorder, and he would not talk about or address his unfaithfulness.

And how did the caller deal with her husband's many problems? As we dug a little deeper, I discovered that this woman had lived with him for twenty years, and she had a pattern of being passive-aggressive—getting angry and blowing up, threatening and not following through. The decision she had to make went far beyond how to communicate with her husband better. Since her passive-aggressive approach was getting her nowhere, what did she need to do now to stop enabling his behavior? It was only after this caller could clearly identify the real problem that she started to address the deeper issues in her marriage.

When you need to be sure you've identified the real decision that needs to be made, stop and ask yourself, What's going on? What are my options? What do I have to do to change or to be the person to make this happen?

2. **Create options.** Old-time comedian Buddy Hackett said, "My mother's menu consisted of two choices: Take it or leave it!" Sometimes that's the way we feel. One caller was trying to decide whether she should open the door and shove her young adult child out.

Here is how she posed the question: "Should I continue to enable my daughter, or should I be a 'meanie'?" I stopped her because she was failing to consider many other options. Isn't it interesting that we go to the store expecting to find fifty different options for toothpaste, but when we face a decision, we are all black-and-white: we must either do this or do that?

When you feel caught between a rock and a hard place, when

neither of two options looks good, ask God for new ideas, new thoughts, and new options. He's very creative! Options are freeing and exciting. So often people say, "I must make a decision today— either yes or no." Doesn't God allow for answers like "Maybe later" or "Before I decide, I need to get more information so I am clear on all my options"?

God's options are not always simply yes or no. Remember what happened after King David disobeyed God, conducting a census in Israel even though that would displease the Lord? Essentially God told him, "David, you disobeyed me. Now I will give you three choices of punishment. You can either have three years of famine, three months of being defeated by your foes, or three days of the sword of the Lord. You pick."

David thought about it and selected the plague, saying, "Let me fall into the hands of the LORD, for his mercy is very great. Do not let me fall into human hands" (1 Chronicles 21:13, NLT). Even though all three options would bring pain, he made a decision—he chose to fall into God's hands.

ONE THING

When you're stuck between two options—neither of which seems very good—talk with a friend, pastor, or counselor to get another perspective on whether other options exist.

Often people think they must choose from one of two not-so-great options. People call the radio program to ask, "Should I divorce or stay with my spouse?" as if those are the only options. They don't consider that instead of a divorce they might consider an intervention, counseling, or separation.

I also talk to many callers who tell me something like, "All I can do is yell at my kids—if I don't, they will get away with whatever they want." Listen, parents: you have several more options to consider.

- You may need to begin applying preset consequences for disobedience.

- You may need to listen to your child's heart.
- Perhaps you and your spouse need to work together to provide consistent discipline.
- You may need to go to a parenting class, read a book, or talk with other parents to get other ideas on discipline.
- You may just need to learn to walk around the block or count to ten before disciplining your child.

3. **Create the plan.** Often by this point we know what we ought to do because we have prayed and thought about it. Yet this is where many people get stuck. They may be afraid, knowing that making any decision can be risky. (Of course, that's true even of getting up and driving to work every day.) Such fear can be alleviated, however, by making a plan before acting on your decision.

Though we're not given all the details, it's clear that after Nehemiah prayed and was given permission to go to Jerusalem to shore up his city's walls, he then had to consider how to deal with the many challenges of rebuilding the wall. He had enemies who were ready to attack. He had resources he had to deploy. He must have explored options—*should we do it this way or that way?* He made the decision and then made a plan.

Let's say you realize that you are yelling at your kids to compensate for what you feel is your spouse's overly tolerant stance toward discipline. You may both be dissatisfied with the results in your home and may agree to begin working together to be more consistent in your approach. That's a great first step, but how will you make this happen? Perhaps you'll discuss the outcomes you both want and expect from your kids and promise not to let your children bypass a no from one parent by going to the other. Once you have a plan in place, it's time to move. Like Nehemiah, you pray, plan, and act.

4. **Act on your plan.** American cowboy and humorist Will Rogers said, "Even if you are on the right track, you will get run over if you just sit there." Once your plan is put together, review these five final steps before acting:

- *Pray about it again!* "God, here I am again. I'm ready to act. Is this right? Please make this clear to me."
- *Pick the right option.* "God, you have generated many options for me. I have gotten good counsel and prayed. Help me to choose the right one."
- *Review your actions.* Have you formulated the specific steps necessary to make your plan happen? Have you gotten the agreement of others involved in carrying out the plan?
- *Proclaim it to the right person.* It's important to ask for prayer support and accountability. Be sure to seek out a trustworthy and wise person.
- *Pounce.* After you have made your decision, prayed about it, put the plan together, and told someone about it, you're like a cat ready to pounce. Now is the time to act on that first step in your plan. This is another part of the decision-making process where many people fall short.

For twenty-plus years, I have worked with couples and families in counseling; as a result, I know that far too few of us ever really make lasting changes. Too many of us are thinking and acting the same way we did five or ten years ago. As a result, the same problems keep coming up. If this describes you, my challenge is that you be clear about the decision you need to make, get help if you need it, pray about it, create options, put a plan together based on the option you choose, and step out in faith and act.

Successful people are intentional about making decisions. They are willing to take risks, even when that is scary. They realize that if they never take a risk, they will never move forward. Unsuccessful people avoid decisions, preferring to let life take them where it will. Their fear of taking risks may almost immobilize them from acting. They would rather have the problems they have today than take a chance on having different, possibly bigger problems tomorrow.

Since we decided to expand our ministry during that difficult time of decision several years ago, we have seen great growth. It hasn't been easy or free of problems, but we took action and we have seen results. As we look back, can we see other options we might have followed or ways we might have done things better? Sure. But we acted, and God has blessed our efforts to take a risk to follow where he was leading us.

ONE SMALL THING TO BEGIN CHANGING YOUR LIFE

- Do you keep encountering the same problem or interpersonal conflict over and over? If so, begin thinking and praying about its root cause. (Refer to chapter 12 for help in formulating the right questions.) Then write out what decision you need to make to overcome this challenge.

- Are you currently weighing just two options as you consider a major decision, assuming it has to be all one way or the other? If so, write down five other options in handling this decision. Ask others to help brainstorm with you if you need help.

- If you already have chosen an option, begin outlining the steps you'll need to take to implement your decision.

- Pray about your decision again, make your choice, tell someone what you've decided, and take the first action step on your plan today.

14
A DREAM WORTH PURSUING

We need men who can dream of things that never were.
—JOHN F. KENNEDY

The day Raj missed his daughter's piano recital was a turning point in his life. Raj, the information services manager you read about in chapter 9, understood that he had missed an important opportunity to support his daughter and strengthen their relationship. His uneasiness grew the following week when he was late for dinner twice. Not surprisingly, his wife was unhappy that his work always seemed to take priority over the family. As they talked about the frustration they both felt, Raj wondered aloud if he really had to live this way. Raj began to pray that God would give him a solution. Slowly a dream was born in his heart and mind.

I started this book by promising that you can overcome your biggest challenge if you understand and apply the power of one thing. Taking just one small step each day will help you develop the character and discipline that will change your life for the better. In this final chapter, I'd like you to consider how the power of one thing works in another way. To do so, you'll need to shift your attention away from issues and challenges and onto your dreams and goals.

I like to think of a dream as a God-inspired vision of a better future resulting in a passionate response of action today. Solomon understood this several millennia ago. *The Message* paraphrases his words of wisdom this way: "If people can't see what God is doing, they stumble all over themselves; but when they attend to what he reveals, they are most blessed" (Proverbs 29:18). Throughout the Bible, we see God planting a dream within men and women that would change their lives and the lives of those around them:

- Noah was given a vision to save all of humankind.
- Abraham was given a vision to father a great nation.
- Joseph was given a dream to save a nation and his family.
- Esther was a given a dream to save her people.

Clearly God used these people to advance his will in significant, world-changing ways. Raj's dream, and probably yours, may not be on that scale. However, all of us can have life-changing dreams—dreams God gives us to shape our lives and the lives of those around us. These are dreams worth pursuing, and they will help us live intentionally.

The Bible presents a number of life-changing dreams that God wants all people to strive for:

- Husbands are to love their wives.
- Wives are to respect their husbands.
- Fathers and mothers are to train up their children in the way they should go, so that when they are old they will not depart from it.
- Employees are to be subject to authority and work hard.
- We are all to love one another just as Christ Jesus has loved us.

If you don't think these items qualify as dreams, just think of what your world would be like if these God-given goals became reality. Raj understood that God's vision for him was to love his wife and keep from exasperating his children. As long as he remained with his company, these goals would seem as out of reach as if he had determined, with no medical knowledge, to find a cure for cancer.

WHAT SEPARATES DOERS FROM DREAMERS?

If you have been unable to progress toward your dream but don't really understand why, I encourage you to picture a rubber band sitting unused on a table or in a drawer. It experiences no stress or tension until someone picks it up and stretches it so it can be used to secure a stack of papers. As it's stretched, the rubber band experiences tension and soon resists being stretched any further. It seems to want to go back to its slack, unused state.

Humans are like that rubber band. Our tendency is to want to stay in our accustomed state. It's always easiest to be like a limp rubber band that is accomplishing nothing. After all, safety and security seem surest when we avoid situations that could lead to failure, insecurity, disapproval—or even ridicule.

Taking just one small step each day will help you develop the character and discipline that will change your life for the better.

People respond to a dream worth pursuing in one of two ways.

Your willingness to do one thing

Some people have a dream and begin working toward it, one small thing at a time. These individuals are committed to acting on their vision; they don't wait for something or someone else to make them successful. They are consistently upbeat and encouraged. That doesn't mean they never get discouraged; however, whenever disappointment knocks them down, they remain focused on their dream. They get up the next morning, ready to do the next one thing and unwilling to dwell on the mistakes, problems, or failures of the previous day.

Consider what would have happened if American inventors had been unwilling to weather the resistance they faced. Back in the 1800s, Napoleon, commenting on Robert Fulton's steamship, said, "What, sir, would you make a ship sail against the wind and currents by lighting a bonfire under her deck? I pray you excuse me; I have no time to listen to such nonsense!"

In 1829, Martin Van Buren said, "Railroad carriages are pulled at the enormous speed of fifteen miles per hour by engines which, in addition to endangering life and limb of passengers, roar and snort their way through the countryside, setting fire to the crops, scaring the livestock, and frightening women and children. The Almighty certainly never intended that people should travel at such breakneck speed."

In 1910, on the brink of World War I, the British secretary of war said, "We do not consider that aeroplanes will be of any possible use for war purposes."

Someone might be saying to you right now, "That's a great idea, but it will never work." Will you accept this comment as truth? Or will you push past this resistance to achieve the dream God has put in your heart?

The second group of people may wish just as fervently that their dreams will come true. However, they are not committed to doing the one thing each day necessary to move them toward their goal. Often they focus more on all the problems and obstacles that stand in their way rather than the next thing they could do to get a little closer. They accept discouragement, defeat, and failure. They often rely on others to make them feel okay.

Will you push past the resistance to achieve the dream God has put in your heart?

They may have good intentions, but their dreams feel elusive. They don't recognize that they have the power to succeed. As Ralph Waldo Emerson said, "Good thoughts are no better than good dreams, unless they are executed."

Which type of dreamer are you? Which of these two types do you want to be? After you've considered this, keep reading. A few more characteristics separate doers from dreamers.

Your view of God

Your view of God will play a big role in how you approach your dream. Two biblical characters—uncle and nephew—had two different views of God, and their lives reflected that. When his uncle Abraham was led by God to leave his homeland, Lot left with him. When they finally stopped and settled, it became clear that both men had so many flocks they would need to separate. Abraham offered Lot the land of his choice. Lot took the best land, putting his security in the property he had chosen. He didn't fully trust or obey God; it seems he thought the Lord's ability and power were limited. Lot had a small view of God.

Abraham not only left Ur, he also entered into a covenant with God. The Lord promised to provide an heir through which a great people would come. Yet many years went by, and Abraham and Sarah remained childless. Eventually, the couple tried to solve their dilemma by human means, and Sarah's servant, Hagar, gave birth to Abraham's son. Yet when God approached Abraham thirteen years later to reaffirm their covenant, Abraham trusted God. Not long after, the son God had promised, Isaac, arrived.

Abraham's greatest test came years later, when God commanded Abraham to lead his son to a mountain where he was to sacrifice Isaac. The very next morning, Abraham prepared for the trip, unsure what God would do but willing to obey him. Of course, God stopped Abraham before he killed his son—but not before Abraham had laid Isaac on the altar. No wonder Abraham has a prominent place in what many Christians call the Faith Hall of Fame:

> It was by faith that Abraham obeyed when God called him to leave home and go to another land that God would give him as his inheritance. He went without knowing where he was going. . . . It was by faith that Abraham offered Isaac as a sacrifice when God was testing him. Abraham, who had received God's promises, was ready to sacrifice his only son, Isaac, even though God had told him, "Isaac is the son through whom your descendants will be counted." Abraham reasoned that if Isaac died, God was able to bring him back to life again. (Hebrews 11:8, 17-19, NLT)

While Abraham faltered whenever he relied on his own wisdom or ingenuity (such as when he lied about Sarah's relationship to him because of his fear of Pharaoh), we don't see Abraham resisting God or arguing with God or complaining to God. He completely trusted God. Abraham's view of God was that he was trustworthy; he was to be obeyed; and he was sovereign. He saw God for who he is, with all of his majesty and power. Abraham had a big view of God.

You may be thinking that your teenager has a small view of your parenting—he or she challenges your authority and insists on going his or her own way. Abraham and Lot demonstrate the difference between a mature view of God (Abraham) and a teenage view of God (Lot).

When it comes to achieving your dream, your view of God makes a crucial difference. If you have a big view of God, you can live with un-certainty because you trust him. You don't have to know everything that is going to happen tomorrow or a year from now because you recognize that God is in control. You aren't afraid to do the next one thing that will take you closer to your dream, knowing that even if things don't turn out the way you pictured, you can trust God to meet your needs and bring good out of difficulties.

If your view of God is more like Lot's, you doubt God's ability or de-sire to come through for you. As a result, you are unwilling to live with uncertainty or to take risks. Your fear and uncertainty paralyze you, and you desperately seek to control all possible outcomes. As a result, you are far less likely to consistently do the one small thing each day necessary to reach your vision.

What is your view of God—do you see him as trustworthy, sover-eign, and to be obeyed? Or are you running from him, believing you can do whatever you want without consequences? This distinction is very important as we now look at whether the dream you have is a dream worth pursuing.

When it comes to achieving your dream, your view of God makes a crucial difference.

In keeping with one of the themes of this book, which is to stay in reality and face the truth, let's talk about how to as-sess your dream to determine whether it's from God and whether it's doable. We're not going to be like Garrison Keillor, who said, "I believe in look-ing reality straight in the eye—and denying it." We're going to look reality in the eye and learn from it.

Your motivation, means, and mind-set

In chapter 6, I introduced the formula I often share with listeners and those I counsel:

$$\text{Expectations} - \text{Reality} = \text{Disappointment}$$

Pastor Erwin Lutzer of Moody Church in Chicago said, "Disappoint-ment is caused by having a wrong focus." He went on to explain that if, for example, we expect a husband or wife to meet all our needs for companionship, friendship, emotional connection, entertainment, ministry, and happiness, we will be disappointed. Only God can fulfill all our needs, and only he should be our true focus.

Before I share a few things for you to consider as you determine whether your dream is doable and from God, allow me to share some of the exciting dreams I've heard from callers over the years:

- To start a small home-based business to supplement the family's income
- To go back to school at age forty-five to finish a degree in nursing
- To start music lessons at age fifty in order to play in the community orchestra
- To get out of debt completely within the next three years
- To be an intentional parent
- To retire and then serve overseas
- To become foster parents
- To start teaching a class at church

The list of possible dreams is as long and creative as the list of people willing to dream. Let's look at some of the factors you should consider as you stretch toward your dream:

- *Stress.* As you go for your dream, let's say the stress is enormous and harms your family, your job, or your health. If this is where you are today, you may feel defeated. Proverbs 13:12 says, "Hope deferred makes the heart sick." While some stress in life is normal and even energizing, stress that keeps you awake night after night or prevents you from being fully present with your family or exhausts you so much that you're too wiped out to go to church costs too much.
- *Motivation.* Why do you want your own business? You might say you want the independence your own business will give you or the added earning potential so you can give your family good things or even so you can fund a new ministry. But is a

desire for comfort or prestige a valid reason for pursuing your dream?

- *Means.* What will it take to achieve this dream? Do you have the education, resources, and time that will make this dream possible?
- *Bible backing.* Have you searched God's Word for what it has to say about your dream? In God's eyes, is this venture worth pursuing?

Let's say you have taken your dream—whatever it is—through these four factors and determined that your dream is both achievable and in keeping with God's Word. Now let's look at the state of your dream and how you are feeling about it today:

- *Committed.* Perhaps your commitment to your dream has started to move reality in the direction you desire and you are encouraged.
- *Ambivalent.* Maybe you have pulled back from your original dream and changed your expectations.
- *Disappointed.* Perhaps you are discouraged and feel like your dream isn't going to happen.

What's the state of your dream? Perhaps your marriage or career isn't what you intended it to be. Or your experience as a parent has not turned out as you had anticipated. Maybe you realize you have hit your professional peak and are beyond the point of building a career, or you had hoped to be at a specific place financially by this time of your life— maybe you thought you would be debt free—and you are not there yet. In such situations, you have had to modify your expectations.

Or perhaps you are committed but discouraged—you keep working on your dream without seeing growth or change. You are not going to give up; you are going to keep pushing forward. Everyone around you may be saying it's time to move on, causing you to feel fatigued and frustrated. But you press on.

So what do you do if your dream hasn't panned out despite your best efforts? Earlier in this chapter we talked about your view of God and how that view impacts your life. Remember Noah and his big view of God that caused him to trust and obey God, and Jonah and his small view of God that sent him flying from God's presence and from the job God had given him to do.

Stress that keeps you awake night after night costs too much.

Besides affecting your relationship with God, your view of him colors your view of your life and your future. And it determines your level of passion about today and its opportunities. If, like Abraham, you have a big view of God, you realize that today matters, that it is a gift from God, and that it is an opportunity for you to make a difference, to do one thing that will improve your life in the future.

A person with a small view of God, like Lot's, sees today as just another day with another to-do list to check off, a bunch of chores to complete until he or she drops exhausted into bed to prepare for the next humdrum day.

Which of these individuals will act with more energy and passion? The one who gets through each day as if on a boring treadmill going nowhere or the person who knows that today is a gift that can be used to make a real difference in the life of someone else? I'll vote for Abraham. How about you?

FROM PASSION TO ACTION

The little character named Yoda in the Star Wars movies wisely challenges Luke Skywalker to step up and become the leader he was intended to be, saying, "Do or do not—there is no try!"

Let's return to Nehemiah, who is a great example of someone who strove for and achieved his dream. He was working in the palace of the Persian king when he heard that the walls of his homeland, Jerusalem, had been burned and destroyed. He could have just shrugged his shoulders, looked at it as someone else's problem, and gone on with his business in the Persian palace. Instead, he allowed a dream to grow in his heart—a dream God had given him for his homeland. He was passionate about the condition of his beloved homeland, and he believed he could make a difference. Instead of thinking, *It's not my problem; someone else will have to deal with it,* Nehemiah made a decision and took action.

One of the first things he did was to *weep* for his suffering people. When was the last time you were moved to tears about anything—in your family, in your marriage relationship, or for your country? Nehemiah was so moved by the situation in his homeland that he sat down and wept. He allowed himself to feel deeply.

Next, Nehemiah *mourned*. In other words, he grieved the loss. He realized his people were hurting, families had been separated, lives had been destroyed—and he mourned. He mourned for the human suffering and for the destruction of the city wall and gates that had protected his people. He also mourned because God was not the centerpiece of the children of Israel at that point.

What have you mourned for in recent weeks or months? Have you mourned for a family that suffered loss or tragedy? Have you mourned for the problems in your family? in your marriage? Mourning is healthy and normal, and it is a recognition of loss that is necessary for healing to begin.

Nehemiah also *fasted*—he didn't eat for a period of time, setting aside his own needs to grow more aware of the needs of his people. When we fast, our hunger reminds us of the reason we are fasting—the issue or problem we are bringing before God in this way. Significant spiritual and physical benefits result from fasting. (Fasting is a biblical discipline, but before fasting, I would encourage you to seek medical advice to make sure that you are physically able to fast.)

Finally, Nehemiah *prayed*. He looked for direction from God, and he was willing to do his part to help solve the problem. If we have a dream worth pursuing, we can be committed, passionate, and sure that it's from God, but it's still not going to happen unless we take action—unless we trust God and step out.

We've already looked at what it's like to get discouraged when you don't see your dream coming true or what it's like to modify your dream and lower your expectations. Now let's look at some of the good things that happen when you take action to make your dream come true:

1. **You have a hope and a future.** Knowing that doing just one small thing today will move you toward your dream, you can proceed with confident expectation into the future.

2. **You have meaning today.** What you do today will eventually show up as a better tomorrow. Life is an accumulation of a lot of little acts, words, and attitudes over an extended period of time.

3. **You have a path to follow.** When you think about the dream God has given you, you ask yourself, *How do I get from here to there?* Then you take small steps today that will get you there tomorrow.

4. **You keep your failures in perspective.** Let's say you live about twenty-seven thousand days (about seventy-five years). During many of those days, you, like me, will experience failure of one kind or another—when you don't accomplish what you intended to do; when you say something you wish you hadn't; when you don't keep your resolution to faithfully exercise, eat healthy, or read your Bible. But because you realize you can start over tomorrow and that God forgives and helps you move forward, you know that your failure isn't final.

5. **You see the big picture more clearly.** Your dream gives you a goal or a finish line to work toward. You know you won't get there in one day, one week, or maybe even one year. But by keeping the dream in mind, you can see the small steps you're taking in the context of the larger vision you're headed for.

6. **You have the opportunity to gain self-discipline.** In Galatians 5, Paul says that the Holy Spirit produces self-discipline, along with other fruit of the Spirit, within believers who follow his leading. Self-discipline will enable you to persevere and get from where you are today to the fulfillment of the dream God has placed in your life. When you understand this, you'll have added incentive to rely on the Spirit to help you develop this critical area of life. If you're a believer, you already have self-discipline available to you—you just need to use it.

7. **You learn to work with others.** You are not going to accomplish your dream alone. All the worthwhile dreams that we see in Scripture and the great things we see done in our communities are always

done in cooperation with others. A mom and dad work together or a single parent gets support in raising his or her children; employees work together to launch a new product; a church works together to build a great congregation. A doable, God-given dream will give you the desire for community and cooperation with others who will help you achieve it.

Raj sought the Lord's direction as he considered how he could make his family a priority while still pursuing his passion and gifts in the area of technology. About six months after beginning his quest, Raj had researched, planned, and taken action to found his own technology company, working with others from around the world from his home. While he still put in many hours, he had more control over when he would work, and since his partners were in India and Europe and in different time zones, he was often able to work at odd hours and be available for his family when they needed him.

If we have a dream worth pursuing, we can be committed, passionate, and sure that it's from God, but it's still not going to happen unless we take action—unless we trust God and step out.

Do you see how the power of one thing expands beyond the challenges you face? Sometimes a problem is just the spark you need to ignite a dream that may have lain dormant in your heart for years. Sometimes it's an idea that strikes you when you're reading or bicycling or working. Other times it's a nudging that tells you God is working in your life.

My prayer is that you will listen to him, get prepared, make a plan, and do one thing today to make your dream come true.

NOTE FROM THE AUTHOR

My parents were married for over fifty years. They were an example to me of the power of one thing to change a life. Committed to each other and to Christ, my parents made a bold decision and acted upon it when I was sixteen years old and still at home. Driven by a dream to make their lives really matter, they sold everything we had in order to start a non-profit ministry committed to doing one thing—reaching needy children with the gospel. Out of their desire to use their remaining days for a purpose that would outlive their lives together, they founded, along with my brother, Larry, and his wife, Cheri, the Youth Haven ministry, a ranch for underprivileged children. Up until the time of their last breath, my mom and dad had one thing on their minds and in their hearts—to serve Christ and model for their children and grandchildren what it means to live an intentional life in Christ.

You, too, can start the journey today. I've given you dozens of "one things" to consider throughout this book. You can start at any point in the process by picking any of the one things you've read as the launching point for the rest of your life. But unless you start by choosing and acting on one thing, your life will be no different tomorrow than it is today.

My passion in life is to support people on the journey toward living an intentional life and to finish strong, as my parents did. I invite you to join us! There's help and encouragement at www.TheIntentionalLife.com.

NOTES

1. "Bad at Multitasking? Blame Your Brain," *Talk of the Nation*, National Public Radio (October 16, 2008), http://www.npr.org/templates/story/story.php?storyId=95784052.
2. If you think such a visible reminder might encourage you to keep at your "one thing," you can visit http://www.TheIntentionalLife.com to find out how to order your own wristband.
3. C. S. Lewis, *Mere Christianity* (New York: HarperCollins, 1952), 227.
4. See http://www.angermanage.co.uk/data.html.
5. Daniel Goleman, *Emotional Intelligence* (New York: Bantam, 1995).
6. M. Scott Peck, *The Road Less Traveled* (New York: Simon & Schuster, 1978), 30.
7. Chip Scanlan, "Tools of the Trade: The Question," Poynter Online, http://www.poynter.org/content/content_view.asp?id=5075&sid=2 (accessed April 1, 2009).
8. John Brady, *The Craft of Interviewing* (New York: Vintage Books, 1977), 37.

THE POWER OF ONE THING
IN ACTION

Information + Insight + Action = Intentional Living

The Problem:

My Goal:

Based on
this *information* (the facts of your situation):

and this *insight* (after prayerfully thinking through the problem):

I commit to this *action* (my one thing):